Creative Hostess Cookbooks

Creative Hostess Cookbooks

To dear Anne,

Here's adding to your
collection! Thanks for
such a lovely stay.

Much love,

Bernard O Bally.

Aug., 1985

The Creative Hostess
CHELTENHAM
AND
GLOUCESTER
COOKBOOK

2

We would like to thank all those who have helped us in the preparation of this book, particularly Mrs Jill Voyce, Gloucestershire County History Librarian and all the restaurateurs and chefs listed on pages 78-80 who have kindly provided us with recipes.

SPOT THE FOX WEATHER VANE *shown on the previous page if you visit Badminton, reputedly the home of foxhunting (see page 59).*

THIS WINCHCOMBE GROTESQUE *is of Ralph Boteler, a former Lord Sudeley (see page 19).*

© Copyright 1985 Marion Edwards Limited

First published 1985 by
Marion Edwards Limited,
69 Abingdon Road,
Kensington W8 6AW

ISBN 0 904330 89 3
Printed in England by
T.J. Press (Padstow) Ltd.
Cornwall

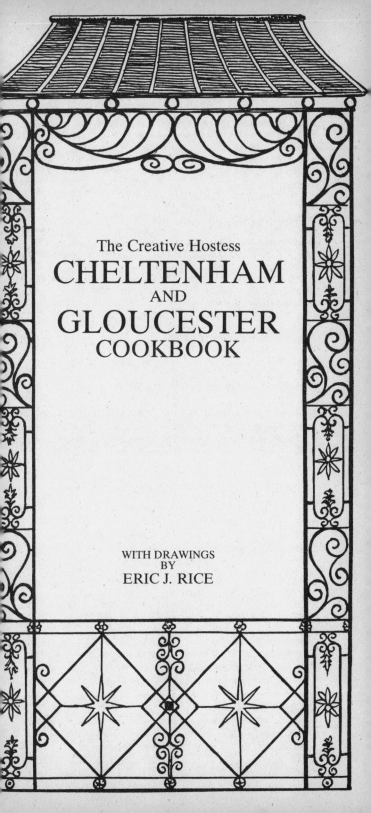

The Creative Hostess

CHELTENHAM
AND
GLOUCESTER
COOKBOOK

WITH DRAWINGS
BY
ERIC J. RICE

Introduction

What immense variety the West Cotswolds has to offer! Its architecture ranges from honey-coloured cottages to Cheltenham's elegant Georgian terraces, from the splendour of Gloucester's magnificent Gothic cathedral to the fascination of its docks. The countryside and villages also offer a wealth of scenic beauty to the visitor, so perhaps it is not surprising that the food offered in the restaurants and hotels is similarly noteworthy.

Chefs throughout the area have willingly parted with their favourite recipes for this volume. If you are lucky enough to live locally or to be on holiday in the West Cotswolds, you will no doubt take time to enjoy some of these dishes prepared by the masters' hands. And when you feel like a treat at home you can recreate their specialities in your own kitchen.

Interspersed between these culinary treats are fascinating facts about the area, together with an artist's view of some of its architectural and scenic gems. Dip into this little memento at your leisure to discover more about the West Cotswolds, and impress your friends by cooking and serving some of the mouth-watering dishes of the region.

A note on measures and conversions

Ingredients are in metric, Imperial (lb/oz) and American measures. **Use measures from one column only**. Teaspoon and tablespoon measures in the metric column correspond to 5 ml and 15 ml respectively. Unless otherwise stated, all fruits and vegetables used should be medium-sized.

YE OLDE FISH SHOPPE, GLOUCESTER

Built around 1535, this busy shop with its stunning timber frame is a fine example of the city's Tudor buildings. The 16th century Raven Tavern next door has now been converted into a club for the elderly.

FISH FIDDLE DE-DEE

Severn salmon are noted for their fine flavour, and elvers, the only fish apart from whitebait allowed to be caught, are a great delicacy. In the past, lampreys were also caught, and were a royal favourite. Indeed, Henry I is said to have died of 'surfeit of lampreys' in 1133. Gloucester, a Royal Town for over 800 years, still presents the monarch with a lamprey pie on Coronation Day. The one sent to Queen Victoria on her Diamond Jubilee weighed 20 lb, its oval crust studded with truffles and crayfish, and its top decorated with a golden crown and sceptre. A pie was baked for Queen Elizabeth's Silver Jubilee.

Contents

The Spa Town of Cheltenham

'The town under the hill' — 'chelt' being Anglo Saxon for cliff and 'ham' meaning settlement — is how early settlers described Cheltenham. But the name gives no indication of the reason why it developed into the prosperous and elegant town we see today.

The discovery of a spring

In 1716, a Quaker farmer, William Mason, noticed that pigeons flocked to his land to peck at the salt crystals, and this led him to discover a spring whose waters had very special properties. The pigeons, incidentally, have not been forgotten — for their important role in discovering Cheltenham spa water they were incorporated into the city symbol, and two stand proudly on its coat of arms.

The site of the spring was inherited by Captain Henry Skillicorne, Mason's son-in-law, who saw the commercial potential and developed the well. Its history can be read on his gravestone in possibly the longest epitaph in any British parish church.

Royal patronage

It was royal patronage which established Cheltenham as a fashionable spa town. In spite of earlier visitors such as **Dr. Johnson**, **Frideric Handel** and **John Wesley**, it remained an ordinary market town until **George III** and his entourage, which

(Footnote!)

GEORGE III was a simple man, noted for his frugality and plain lifestyle and not least for his sometimes eccentric behaviour. One story told of him meeting a local farmer with his herd of sheep outside the town. After discussing the price of livestock, the farmer asked if he had seen the king, whom he understood to dress very plainly. "Aye," the king is said to have replied, "as plain as you see me now."

7

CHELTENHAM IRONWORK — *see left and page 3* — *is an important feature of its architecture. The Georgian terrace unified several homes into one design, and most are of Greek revival. Sadly, many of the town's beautiful railings and gates were removed for making munitions in the Second World War. Even more sadly, it is now believed that this was largely a propaganda exercise, and that many such beautiful examples of the blacksmith's art were simply left to rust away.*

included the novelist **Fanny Burney**, began to visit Cheltenham regularly. Its popularity as a spa was confirmed with newspapers of the day declaring, *"all fashions are completely Cheltenhamized"*.

It did not take long for the town to take shape, and since there was no medieval site to curtail well-planned development, the new streets were wide and graceful. The foundations were laid of the elegant modern town we see today, its streets lined with chestnut, lime, larch and cedar trees, and with 200 acres of parks and open spaces.

A centre of learning

Cheltenham flourished during the 19th century and soon established itself as a centre of education, literature, and the arts. Today it boasts three public schools, two Church of England colleges, a technical college, and an art college.

Continued on page 10...

TAKING THE WATERS

'Muriate of soda, sulphates of soda, lime and magnesia, oxide of iron, chloride of magnesium and iodine and bromide' await anyone who wishes to 'take the waters' at Cheltenham. Acclaimed in the last century for their wide curative powers, they were particularly recommended for liver and digestive complaints picked up in India — leading many old soldiers to retire in the town.

Pumps, like the one in the Town Hall, are still in use today for those with faith and strong stomachs! The Town Hall is 80 years old, and boasts an impressively columned Great Hall.

THE PROMENADE

Cheltenham's most fashionable thoroughfare is lined with chestnut trees and imposing shops, epitomising the elegance and grandeur of a Regency spa town. The Fountain of Neptune stands alongside a bronze statue of Edward Adrian Wilson, the Antarctic explorer.

Continued from page 7...

Cheltenham College was one of the first Victorian public schools, and one of its early masters was the former Poet Laureate, **Cecil Day Lewis**. He found the atmosphere of the school so stuffy that he clashed frequently with its authorities — even for not allowing him to paint his house wearing a green shirt.

The early days of **Cheltenham Ladies College** were less restrained, with dog fights in the classroom — pets were allowed to be kept in the cloakrooms. Order was restored under Miss Dorothea Beale who, as Principal, expanded the pupilage from 69 to a thousand, and so establishing the largest girls' boarding school in the world. Discipline under Miss Beale was necessarily strict, with a strict rule of silence broken for only 20 minutes each morning. This led to the now famous rhyme:

> *"Miss Buss and Miss Beale*
> *Cupid's dart do not feel.*
> *How different from us,*
> *Miss Beale and Miss Buss."*

Culture and sport

The Cheltenham Music and Literature Festivals are now world famous, taking place in July and October respectively. The first Music Festival was held in 1945, four years before its Edinburgh counterpart, and many 'firsts' in the music world have been scored here. Perhaps Cheltenham's most famous musician was the composer **Gustav Holst**, who is known to millions for his composition 'The Planets Suite'. Born in 1874, his house in Clarence Road has been converted into the Gustav Holst Birthplace Museum.

No history of Cheltenham would be complete without mentioning the racecourse. The annual battle for the **Cheltenham Gold Cup** is a classic in the racing calendar, and many renowned international jockeys such as **Fred Archer** and **George Stevens** were local stable lads.

MONTPELLIER WALK

Leading off the far end of the Promenade, this charming walk was built by W.H. Knight in 1840. The shopfronts are supported by a row of Greek caryatides, three of which were sculpted in terracotta by Rossi. The rest were made in stone by W. Brown of Tivoli Street.

Starters

ARTICHOKE AND TOMATO SOUP *Serves 4*

God's in his heaven, all's right with the world – especially when you've just enjoyed this cream-topped soup served at the Gloucester Cathedral Refectory.

Metric		lb/oz	U.S.A.
	500 g (1 lb) Jerusalem artichokes		
1	Large onion	1	1
30 g	Butter	1 oz	2 tbsp
30 g	Flour	1 oz	¼ cup
225 g	Tomatoes, can of	8 oz	1 cup
1	Garlic clove, crushed	1	1
½	Orange, juice and rind of	½	½
1	Bay leaf	1	1
700 ml	Chicken stock	1¼ pt	3 cups
1 tbsp	Cornflour	1 tbsp	1 tbsp
4 tbsp	Single cream	4 tbsp	⅓ cup

1. Slice the artichokes and chop the onion finely. Heat the butter in a large pan and cook the vegetables until soft but not browned. Remove from the heat and stir in the flour.
2. Add the tomatoes, garlic, orange rind tied with the bay leaf, and stock. Season with salt and freshly ground black pepper. Stir until boiling, then cover and simmer for about 20 minutes until the artichokes are very tender.
3. Remove the bay leaf and orange rind, and liquidize or sieve the soup. Return to the rinsed out pan, add the orange juice, season to taste and simmer gently.
4. Thicken with cornflour slaked in a little cold water, if necessary, then stir in the cream.

GLOUCESTER'S SOUTHGATE STREET CLOCK *dates from 1904. With the help of an Irish colleen, John Bull, a Scottish piper and a Welsh maid, Father Time strikes the quarters.*

THE PITTVILLE PUMP ROOM

Built by the Georgian entre-preneur Joseph Pitt in 1825, the Pittville Pump Room is the centrepiece of a splendid estate. A flourishing social life evolved throughout the 'season'. There was the daily routine of taking the waters in the morning, and walks, rides, and concerts in the pleasure grounds in the afternoon.

With a general loss of interest in spa towns and its out-of-town location, Pittville eventually declined in popularity — despite such appealing entertainments as female rope climbers and 'an exhibition of a stupendous elephant swimming in the lake'.

Today the well-restored building houses a Costume Museum, and is used for private functions and events connected with Cheltenham's Music and Literature Festivals.

CARROT AND ORANGE SOUP   *Serves 6*

Quick and easy to make, this Gloucester Cathedral Refectory soup is both tasty and colourful.

Metric		lb/oz	U.S.A.
1	Onion, chopped	1	1
30 g	Butter	1 oz	2 tbsp
425 g	Carrots, can of	15 oz	15 oz
850 ml	Chicken stock	1½ pt	3½ cups
200 ml	Frozen orange juice, can of	⅓ pt	¾ cup
225 ml	Single cream	8 fl. oz	1 cup
	Chives to garnish		

1. Cook the onion in the butter until soft but not browned.
2. Drain the carrots and liquidize or sieve with the onion and a little of the stock.
3. Return the carrot purée to the pan, add the remaining stock, orange juice and cream. Heat slowly to just below boiling point.
4. Season to taste and serve garnished with snipped chives.

ICED FENNEL SOUP WITH ALMONDS
Serves 4

Toasted almonds folded into lightly whipped cream add the finishing touch to this delicious and unusual iced soup served at the Gentle Gardener Hotel in Tetbury.

Metric		lb/oz	U.S.A.
	1 Head of fennel, sliced		
150 ml	*Dry white wine*	¼ pt	½ cup
45 g	*Ground almonds*	1½ oz	½ cup
	Ground ginger, pinch of		
4 tbsp	*Double or whipping cream*	4 tbsp	⅓ cup
1 tbsp	*Flaked almonds, toasted*	1 tbsp	1 tbsp

1. Place the fennel in 750 ml (1¼ pt, 3 cups) of water with the wine. Simmer for 20 minutes until tender.
2. Purée the mixture and stir in the ground almonds and ginger. Season to taste. Simmer for a further 15 minutes, then chill until ready to serve.
3. Just before serving, lightly whip the cream, fold in the almonds and put a spoonful on top of each bowl of soup.

> "Here lie I and my four daughters
> Killed by drinking Cheltenham waters,
> Had we but stuck to Epsom Salts,
> We wouldn't have been in these here vaults."
>
> (Reputedly a one-time epitaph in St. Mary's Church-yard, Cheltenham)

14

HOT AVOCADO WITH CRAB — *Serves 4*

A luxury starter from Below Stairs in Cheltenham.

Metric		lb/oz	U.S.A.
	2 Ripe avocados		
175 g	Crabmeat	6 oz	1 cup
	Cayenne pepper, dash of		
60 g	Butter, softened	2 oz	¼ cup
1	Garlic clove, crushed	1	1
	Deep-fried parsley sprigs and hot toast to garnish		

1. Make the garlic butter well in advance. Beat the butter and garlic together and season well with salt and freshly ground black pepper. Transfer on to a butter paper and mould into a cylinder*, then refrigerate.
2. Set the grill to its highest setting, then halve, peel and stone the avocados. Slice each half from the thick end, and spread out like fans on an ovenproof dish. Cover with the crabmeat, and season with salt, freshly ground black pepper and a dash of cayenne.
3. Make the toast and deep-fry the parsley sprigs for a few seconds, then top the crabmeat with a round of garlic butter and place under the grill to glaze and heat through.
4. Serve garnished with the parsley and toast.

* Shape roughly with a knife, then roll in the wrapper.

MARINATED MUSHROOMS WITH PRAWNS — *Serves 6-8*

*'Grow. Grow. Grow little mushrooms grow.
Somebody wants you soon.'*

A speciality of the Burleigh Court at Minchinhampton.

Metric		lb/oz	U.S.A.
	700 g (1½ lb) Button mushrooms		
350 g	Peeled prawns	12 oz	2 cups
1	Large lemon, juice of	1	1
450 ml	Wine vinegar	¾ pt	1¾ cups
1	Garlic clove, crushed	1	1
2	Onions, chopped	2	2
1	Bouquet garni	1	1
300 ml	Olive oil	½ pt	1 cup
1½ tbsp	Tomato ketchup	1½ tbsp	1½ tbsp
3 tbsp	Chopped parsley to garnish	3 tbsp	¼ cup

1. Wipe and clean the mushrooms, and put into a pan with the lemon juice and just enough water to cover. Bring to the boil, simmer for 5 minutes, then leave to cool.

2. Put the vinegar into a pan and add the garlic, onions, and bouquet garni. Season with salt and freshly ground black pepper. Boil, uncovered, for 5 minutes, then leave to cool. Stir in the olive oil and tomato ketchup.
3. Drain the mushrooms well and put them into a deep bowl. Pour the dressing over and leave to marinate for several hours, or overnight, in the refrigerator.
4. To serve, remove the mushrooms with a slotted spoon and place them in a shallow serving dish. Arrange the prawns on top, strain the dressing over, and sprinkle with parsley.

GARLIC BREAD   *Serves 8-10*

Popular at Cheltenham's Montpellier Wine Bar, understandably!

1. Set the oven to 210°C, 425°F, Gas Mark 7, and cut a French stick into thick slices. Beat 6 crushed cloves of garlic and 4 tbsp of chopped parsley into 225 g (8 oz/1 cup) butter and season with salt and freshly ground black pepper.
2. Spread on the slices, 'reform' into a loaf and wrap up well in foil. Bake for 5-10 minutes and serve at once.

COLD TERRINE OF FRESH CRAB   *Serves 6*

The Corse Lawn House Hotel serves this seafood starter.

Metric		lb/oz	U.S.A.
	2 Freshly cooked crabs, about 1 kg (2 lb) each		
500g	Monkfish tails, chopped	1 lb	1 lb
6	Pancakes	6	6
2	Egg whites	2	2
1 tbsp	Chives, chopped	1 tbsp	1 tbsp
1 tbsp	Parsley, chopped	1 tbsp	1 tbsp
	Nutmeg, pinch of		
75 ml	Double cream	2½ fl. oz	1 cup
600 ml	Hollandaise sauce (see p. 75)	1 pt	2 cups

1. Extract the meat from the crabs, keeping the white and dark meat separate. Line a terrine about 15 cm (6") long with the pancakes, allowing them to overhang the sides.
2. Set the oven to 210°C, 425°F, Gas Mark 7.
3. Place the monkfish in the blender with the egg whites, herbs, salt, pepper and a good pinch of nutmeg. Blend until smooth and stir in the cream.
4. Layer the monkfish mixture in the terrine with the white and dark crabmeat, starting and finishing with monkfish. Fold the pancakes over the top and cover with the lid or foil. Place in a roasting tin half full of hot water and bake for about 1 hour until firm.
5. Remove the terrine from the oven and put a heavy weight on top to press it while it cools. Serve chilled, cut into slices and accompanied with Hollandaise sauce.

HOT SOLE AND TROUT TERRINE
WITH HERB SAUCE
Serves 15-20

The chef of the Painswick Hotel makes full use of his processor in the preparation of this aromatic dish. If making half the quantity in a smaller terrine, still cook the dish for the same amount of time.

Metric		lb/oz	U.S.A.
500 g	Fresh lemon sole, filleted and skinned*	1 lb	1 lb
250 g	Fresh trout, filleted and skinned*	8 oz	8 oz
250 g	Fresh spinach, blanched and drained	8 oz	8 oz
3	Egg whites	3	3
900 ml	Single cream	1½ pt	3½ cups
	For the herb sauce:		
600 ml	Fish stock (see p. 75)	1 pt	2½ cups
2 tbsp	Noilly Prat	2 tbsp	2 tbsp
150 ml	Double cream	¼ pt	½ cup
	Fresh chives, chervil and dill, roughly chopped, 1 tsp of each		
60 g	Butter	2 oz	¼ cup

1. Butter a 30 cm (12″) long terrine and line with some of the spinach leaves.
2. Put the lemon sole in a food processor fitted with a cutter attachment. Chop finely, add a pinch of salt and 2 egg whites. Process for a further 10 seconds. Add two-thirds of the cream, a little at a time. Turn the mixture into a bowl and season to taste.
3. Repeat the process with the trout using the remaining cream and egg white. Cover the bowls and leave both mixtures on ice for an hour.
4. Set the oven to 180°C, 350°F, Gas Mark 4.
5. Put half the sole mousse into the terrine, spreading evenly. Cover with trout mousse, then the remaining sole and finally spinach leaves.
6. Cover the terrine with buttered foil and bake for about 35-40 minutes until a knife comes out clean when inserted. Allow to cool.
7. Make the herb sauce just before serving. Reduce the fish stock and Noilly Prat by two-thirds. Add the cream and simmer gently to reduce by half. Mix in the herbs and butter and season to taste.
8. Cut the terrine into slices and re-heat in a moderate oven on a buttered dish, moistened with Noilly Prat and covered with tin foil. Be very careful not to overheat or the terrine will dry up and become rubbery.
9. Serve the terrine with the herb sauce.

* Do not use frozen fish – it makes a watery terrine.

THE PARISH CHURCH OF ST. MARY

The only surviving medieval building in Cheltenham, St. Mary's contains some 14th century stained glass windows and numerous memorial plaques, many illustrating Cheltenham's ties with Imperial India. Also commemorated is the Reverend Francis Close, 1826-1858 (the 'Pope of Cheltenham', as Tennyson called him) who was an active 'purist' campaigner and influential in establishing the Cheltenham Colleges.

John Wesley preached at St. Mary's in 1744, but was unimpressed with his congregation, noting ''it was as if I was talking Greek to them''.

Winchcombe

A quiet Cotswolds town today, Winchcombe was once the Saxon capital of Wincelcumbeshire — a thriving walled city, whose Abbot sat in the Anglo Saxon Parliament. The town grew up around its Abbey, which was founded by **Kenulf, King of Mercia** in the 8th century.

During the 16th century the town prospered from tobacco growing, for which its damp, mild climate was ideal. Legend has it that some of the first tobacco in England was planted here by **Sir Walter Raleigh**, and by the mid 17th century much of the neighbouring fields were covered in the 'fragrant weed'. Not all were in favour, and James I detested pipe smoking describing it as "a custom loathsome to the eye, harmful to the brain and dangerous to the lungs". Opposition also came from merchants importing tobacco through Bristol, and troops were eventually sent into Winchcombe with orders, according to Samuel Pepys *"to spoil the tobacco there, which the people do plant contrary to the law and always have done"*.

KENELM, *Kenulf's 7-year old son and widely believed murdered by his sister, Quendrida, is at the centre of a fascinating legend. When his body was brought to Winchcombe to be buried, it rested on Sudeley Hill and was thought to be the cause of a freshwater spring that had miraculous healing powers. A chapel was subsequently built to Kenelm on the spot, which in medieval times rivalled the tomb of Thomas à Beckett as a place for pilgrimage. However, Kenelm's sister did not fare too well in contrast to her saintly brother. On hearing people muttering outside her window one day, she leant out in anger, reciting Psalm 109 backwards, upon which it is said her eyes were torn out by divine retribution.*

SUDELEY CASTLE

THE WINCHCOMBE GROTESQUES *(see page 2)*

The Parish Church of St. Peter, Winchcombe, is famous for its forty gargoyles. Half of these fascinating waterspouts are devils, and the rest are probably caricatures of local dignitaries, such as the helmeted head of Ralph Boteler, a former Lord Sudeley. Inside the church is an altar cloth that is said to have been embroidered by Henry VIII's first wife, Catherine of Aragon.

SUDELEY CASTLE

Just outside Winchcombe lies Sudeley Castle, an impressive building founded 800 years ago, but entirely re-built in 1450. Once the home of Catherine Parr, sixth and sole surviving wife of Henry VIII, Sudeley has witnessed many Royal events and visits over the years. Queen Elizabeth stayed here in 1592 for three days of feasting, pageants and masques, and during the Civil War, Charles I made his headquarters here. Today, visitors can view its needlework tapestries, furniture and paintings, enjoy the regular exhibitions of period costumes, or stroll through the formal gardens and parkland.

THE CHANDOS ALMSHOUSES *at Winchcombe were built in 1573 by Lady Chandos, when resident of nearby Sudeley Castle. When the town was a busy weaving and clothmaking centre, house doors would be left open, because the weavers' guild rules stipulated that no weaver should work in secret, hence the vogue for 'stable' doors.*

HOT MOUSSELINE OF VEGETABLES
WITH CHORON SAUCE   *Serves 6*

This very pretty dish comes from the Corse Lawn Hotel, not far from Gloucester.

Metric		lb/oz	U.S.A.
1.4 kg	Leaf spinach	3 lb	3 lb
1	Whole celeriac	1	1
500 g	Spring carrots	1 lb	1 lb
9	Egg whites	9	9
425 ml	Double cream	¾ pt	1¾ cup
	Nutmeg, coriander and paprika		
	Choron sauce (see page 74)		

1. Prepare and cook each vegetable until just tender. Leave to cool. Set the oven to 220°C, 450°F, Gas Mark 8.
2. One at a time, place each vegetable in a blender goblet with three egg whites and blend until smooth. Place each mixture in a bowl set over crushed ice, stirring in one-third of the cream. Season the celeriac with nutmeg, the carrot with coriander, the spinach with paprika, and all three with salt and pepper.
3. Butter 18 small heatproof moulds, six for each vegetable, and fill. Put in a large roasting tin half-filled with hot water and bake until set, about 12 minutes. Meanwhile, make the sauce and keep warm.
4. Turn out one of each mousseline on to 6 warmed plates and surround with the sauce.

> BELLRINGING *has long been a Gloucester tradition, and* **bell-founding**, *using iron from the nearby Forest of Dean, was one of the city's major industries up to the nineteenth century.*

TERRINE DE LEGUMES FROID
AU COULIS DE TOMATES   *Serves 6-8*

The Close Hotel Chef uses a colourful selection of vegetables for this dish, choosing from carrots, courgettes, broccoli, leeks, swede, artichokes, French beans and mange tout.

Metric		lb/oz	U.S.A.
300 g	Vegetables (see above)	10 oz	2½ cups
250 g	Raw chicken, minced twice	8 oz	2 cups
250 ml	Double cream	8 fl. oz	1 cup
	For the sauce:		
4	Tomatoes	4	4
125 ml	Wine vinegar	4 fl. oz	½ cup
250 ml	Oil	8 fl. oz	1 cup
375 ml	Chicken stock	12 fl. oz	1½ cups
175 g	Tomato purée, can of	6 oz	6 oz

1. Put the chicken into a mixing bowl over ice. Slowly mix in the cream using a spatula.
2. Clean and cut the vegetables into thin strips. Blanch (plunge briefly into boiling water) and leave to cool.
3. Set the oven to 140°C, 275°F, Gas Mark 1.
4. Layer the chicken and vegetables in a deep terrine, starting and ending with chicken.
5. Half-fill a roasting tin with hot water, place the terrine in it and bake for 45 minutes or until the meat and vegetables are tender. Cool and refrigerate.
6. To make the sauce, blanch, skin and de-seed the tomatoes. Put all the sauce ingredients into a liquidizer, season well, adding a pinch of sugar and blend for 10 seconds.
7. Serve the terrine in slices with the sauce poured over.

CHICKEN AND HERB TERRINE WITH ONION MARMALADE
Serves 15-20

A wonderful combination of flavours from the Painswick Hotel.

Metric		lb/oz	U.S.A.
	2 kg (4½ lb) Chicken*		
1 kg	Streaky bacon rashers	2 lb	2 lb
1	Egg white	1	1
600 ml	Single cream	1 pt	2½ cups
60 g	Tarragon, chopped	2 oz	½ cup
60 g	Parsley, chopped	2 oz	½ cup
60 g	Sage, chopped	2 oz	½ cup
60 g	Shallots, finely chopped	2 oz	½ cup
150 ml	Chicken stock or consommé, chilled	½ pt	1 cup
	Onion marmalade (see p. 74)		

1. Make the onion marmalade well in advance.
2. Line a 30 cm (12") long terrine with the de-rinded bacon, reserving some to cover the terrine later.
3. Bone and skin the chicken legs. Chop finely in a food processor with a cutter attachment. Add a pinch of salt and the egg white. Process for a further 20 seconds, then add the cream gradually. Sieve the mixture into a bowl and season to taste. Cover and set over crushed ice for 1 hour.
4. Set the oven to 180°C, 350°F, Gas Mark 4.
5. Skin the chicken breasts and cut lengthwise into thin pieces. Divide the chicken pieces, mousse, herbs and shallots into two. Layer the mousse, herbs, shallots, and breasts moistened with stock, into the terrine, seasoning each layer with pepper. Seal with the remaining bacon.
6. Cover with a lid or buttered foil, and bake for 40 minutes.
7. Serve hot or cold, and offer the onion marmalade separately.

* Preferably maize-fed – these are well-flavoured birds with yellow flesh.

The Royal City of Gloucester

First named by the Celts 'Caer Glow' — the splendid and beautiful city — this ancient gateway to the West was populated by Britons long before the Romans arrived.

The proverb *'scratch Gloucestershire and find Rome'* is certainly true, and no other English city still stands more precisely on its Roman street pattern. The four main streets — North, East, South and Westgate — are in the shape of a cruciform or cross, and fragments of the old **Roman Wall** can still be seen today — there is a viewing chamber in King's Walk.

> WITCOMBE ROMAN VILLA
> *four miles south east of Gloucester, was first discovered in 1818 by workmen digging up an ash tree. Dating back to the end of the first century AD, it has a hypocaust system and several mosaic pavements.*

Saxon and Norman times

In 681 AD, King Ethelred granted the city to **Osric**, Prince of Mercia. The Monastery and Abbey of St. Peter, which preceded the present building, was begun the same year, but it was in the reign of **William Rufus** that work began in earnest on the Cathedral. Together with **Abbot Serlo**, he was responsible for erecting the enormous Norman peers which dominate the nave. The building reached its present beauty and dimensions in the mid-15th century.

 THE FORTRESS OF GLEVUM *was established by the Romans at Gloucester because it was the lowest crossing point of the River Severn. But it was after Elizabeth I granted it port status in 1580 that trade really boomed. A canal was constructed to enable large ships to travel freely between the port and the estuary — the narrow, winding river only being navigable for a few days each month.*

Royal connections

Gloucester has been the stage for many royal occasions, some sad, others joyous. Edward the Confessor chose the city as one of his assembly places in 1081, and began the custom of bringing the Court to Gloucester every Christmas. This continued until the reign of Henry I. In 1216, Henry III was crowned king in the Abbey Church, the first monarch since the Norman invasion to have his Coronation outside London. Ironically, he was later imprisoned in the city by Simon de Montfort.

Richard III, formerly Duke of Gloucester, granted the city a Charter on which much of our local government is based to this day.

During the Civil War, Gloucester threw its support behind the Roundheads — an act that changed the course of history. When Charles I lay siege to the city in 1643, Gloucester's townsfolk made a spirited defence under one Colonel Massey,

Continued on page 26...

ST. JOHN'S STEEPLE

You may be puzzled by this odd stone edifice when passing through St. Lucy's Garden on your way to visit Gloucester Cathedral. It is the spire top from the nearby 14th century Church of St. John the Baptist, removed for safety reasons.

ST LUCY'S GARDEN *is named after the home of charity for orphans and young ladies which once occupied the site. It also contains part of the old city wall.*

"Doctor Foster
Went to Gloucester
In a shower of rain.
He stepped in a puddle
Right up to his middle,
And never went there again."

CATHEDRAL
REFECTORY
OPEN
GOOD FOOD

CHURCH
HOUSE

GLOUCESTER CATHEDRAL

*One of the finest examples of Gothic architecture in England,
the present Cathedral was begun in the reign of William Rufus,
son of William the Conqueror, on the site of an earlier Abbey
which was destroyed by fire in 1058. Among many outstanding
features are the Cloisters, with their magnificent fan vaulting.*

THE GLOUCESTERSHIRE REGI-
MENT'S COLOURS *hanging high in
Gloucester Cathedral were carried
into battle from the Crimean to the
Second World War. The Chapel of
St. Edmund the King houses mem-
orials to both the Gloucestershire
Regiment and Royal Gloucester-
shire Hussars.*

*"A moth eaten rag on a worm eaten pole
It does not look likely to stir a man's soul
'Tis the deeds that were done 'neath the moth eaten rag,
When the pole was a staff and the rag was a flag"*
(From notes on the colours in Gloucester Cathedral)

INSIDE GLOUCESTER CATHEDRAL
*Superb examples of major architectural styles can be seen
inside the Cathedral. Shown here are Norman round-shaped
piers and the Gothic pointed arch in the Nave.*

Continued from page 23
and despite being heavily outnumbered and short of food, the
city survived for almost a month before parliamentarian
reinforcements arrived to relieve the beleaguered city.
After the Restoration, Gloucester's castle and walls were torn
down by Charles II as an act of revenge, but this acted to the
city's advantage, for it allowed Gloucester to expand and grow.

A transport and industrial centre
With its good communications and strategic location, Gloucester made an ideal stopping-off place for travellers and
centre for industry. The coming of the railway added to its
popularity — although it also became the centre of conflict
between the Great Western and Midland Railway Companies
— the inconvenience of having to change from one gauge to
another led to 60 years of bitterness.
The opening of a canal system in 1827 lessened the city's
dependence on the shifting sands of the estuary and boosted
growth. The system stretched from Gloucester to Sharpness,
and the port soon became a rival to nearby Bristol. Huge dock
warehouses were built to cope with the increased traffic from
the industrial centres of South Wales, and it was only when the
Severn tunnel was opened in 1885 that trade declined.
Iron ore and timber from the nearby Forest of Dean played a
part in attracting blacksmiths and ironworkers to set up business. Bell-founding, pin-making and aircraft construction have
all provided employment and added to the city's growth.

Gloucester in the eighties
The importance of the city's location and its royal and religious
connections are still relevant. Tourists come in their thousands
every year, and business and commerce thrive to this day.

TOMATO, MELON AND GRAPE VINAIGRETTE   *Serves 4*

Combine tablespoons of clear honey, cider vinegar, olive oil
and chopped mint in the ratio 2:4:3:1 to make the dressing for
this starter from Tasters Wine Bar.

Metric		lb/oz	U.S.A.
	2 Small melons		
	4 Tomatoes		
175 g	Black grapes, de-seeded	6 oz	1½ cups
1 tbsp	Sesame seeds, toasted	1 tbsp	1 tbsp
	Mint sprigs to garnish		

1. Cut the melons in half and discard the seeds. Scoop out the
   flesh with a melon baller, reserving the skins. Peel, quarter
   and de-seed the tomatoes, mix with the melon and grapes
   and divide between the skins.
2. Immediately before serving, shake the dressing well, pour a
   tablespoon over each, sprinkle with sesame seeds and
   garnish with a sprig of mint.

William, Duke of Normandy, *is buried before the High Altar, and
the Cathedral was also the final resting place of the murdered
Edward II.*
It is believed that the birth of the **Domesday Book** *took place in the
Chapter House. It was 900 years ago, in 1085, that* **William the
Conqueror** *held one of his best known Witans (Great Councils) at
Gloucester, and decreed that this invaluable historical record
should be created.*

PASTA BAZILIQUE   *Serves 4*

A Mediterranean starter from Twelve Suffolk Parade,
Cheltenham.

Metric		lb/oz	U.S.A.
225 g	Pasta shells	8 oz	2 cups
350 g	Gruyère cheese	12 oz	3 cups
300 ml	Olive oil	½ pt	1 cup
2	Garlic cloves, crushed	2	2
½	Lemon, juice of	½	½
10	Basil leaves, chopped	10	10
45 g	Pine kernels	1½ oz	½ cup
	Chopped basil or parsley to garnish		

1. To make the pestou sauce, put the cheese into a liquidizer
   and blend in the oil very slowly until absorbed. Continue to
   blend and add the garlic, lemon, basil and kernels. Season to
   taste.
2. Cook the pasta according to the packet instructions. Strain
   and rinse in hot water to remove excess starch.
3. Return the pasta to the pan over a low heat. Add the sauce,
   stirring thoroughly. Cook till the cheese becomes stringy.
4. Serve at once, garnished with basil or parsley.

RASPBERRY GALANTINE
Serves 2

The Chef of the Queens Hotel, Cheltenham, adds a little raspberry jelly if he has some to hand when making the sauce for this starter or lunch dish.

Metric		lb/oz	U.S.A.
	1 Duck suprême		
60 g	Duck pâté	2 oz	¼ cup
125 g	Raspberries	4 oz	½ cup
2 tbsp	White wine vinegar	2 tbsp	2 tbsp

1. Set the oven to 180°C, 350°F, Gas Mark 4.
2. Make an incision lengthwise in the duck breast to create a pocket, and fill with pâté.
3. Wrap up in well-buttered foil and poach in hot water in the oven for 20-25 minutes. Allow to cool.
4. Meanwhile, place the raspberries in a liquidizer or blender. Add the wine vinegar and blend until you have a purée.
5. Remove the galantine from the foil and coat with the raspberry purée.

SNAILS BLACK TULIP STYLE
Serves 4-6

A house speciality from this popular Cheltenham restaurant.

Metric		lb/oz	U.S.A.
	24 Snails, shelled		
12	5 cm (2") Vol-au-vents	12	12
60 g	Butter	2 oz	¼ cup
125 g	Mushrooms, finely chopped	4 oz	1 cup
2	Garlic cloves, crushed	2	2
3 tbsp	Brandy	3 tbsp	¼ cup
300 ml	Whipping cream	½ pt	1 cup
	Chopped parsley to garnish		

1. Set the oven to 210°C, 425°F, Gas Mark 7.
2. Put the puff pastry cases in the oven for 15-18 minutes to heat through. Discard the lids and remove any soft centre.
3. Meanwhile, melt the butter in a small, heavy frying pan. Add the mushrooms and garlic and fry lightly. Add the snails and toss in the butter until hot.
4. Pour in the brandy and flambé. While still flaming, pour in the cream and simmer gently until reduced to a thick sauce. Remove from the heat.
5. Spoon 2 snails into each of the hot pastry cases and pour the remaining sauce over. Garnish with chopped parsley.

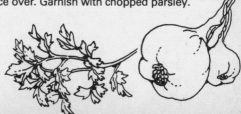

THE HOUSE OF THE TAILOR OF GLOUCESTER

This tiny dwelling was chosen by Beatrix Potter for her old tailor in the children's story, 'The Tailor of Gloucester'. Bought by her publishers in 1979, it has been completely renovated and now houses a shop and museum devoted to Beatrix and the characters she created. Upstairs there is a working model of the mice diligently finishing the Mayor's wedding coat and waistcoat.

CHICKEN LIVER CROUTONS   Serves 4

"Women eat when they talk, men talk when they eat."

MALCOLM DE CHAZALL

Serve this Cleeveway House delicacy as a starter or savoury — either way it will win compliments all round!

Metric		lb/oz	U.S.A.
225 g	*Chicken livers, halved*	8 oz	2 cups
4	*Slices of thick bread*	4	4
	Oil for frying		
60 g	*Butter*	2 oz	¼ cup
16	*Black grapes, de-seeded*	16	16
125 ml	*Port*	4 fl. oz	½ cup
75 ml	*Double cream*	2 fl. oz	¼ cup
1 tsp	*Beef stock*	1 tsp	1 tsp
	Chopped parsley to garnish		

1. Remove crusts from bread and fry in a little hot oil until crisp and lightly browned. Cut into triangles, place on a serving dish and keep warm.
2. Melt the butter in a pan. Add the livers and season with salt and freshly ground black pepper. Seal on both sides.
3. Add the grapes and port and cook for 2 minutes. Pour in the cream and beef stock and simmer very gently, stirring occasionally until reduced to a thick sauce. Season to taste.
4. Pour over the croûtons and serve garnished with parsley.

 BEATRIX POTTER *was born into a well-to-do Victorian family, and developed an early enthusiasm for animals, keeping a variety of pets from rabbits to bats. From her drawings and watercolours grew the stories that became world-famous. The first, 'The Tale of Peter Rabbit', developed from a picture letter she sent to her former governess's young son.*

Although Beatrix brought so much happiness to others, her own early life was tinged with sadness, when her fiancé, Norman, son of her publisher Frederick Warne, died suddenly. But in 1913, at the age of 47, she found happiness with William Heelis, the manager of her farm in the Lake District.

NUTTY PEARS   *Serves 4*

Fruity, creamy, spicy and nutty – a lovely combination from the kitchens of Below Stairs in Cheltenham.

Metric		lb/oz	U.S.A.
	4 Large ripe pears		
60 g	Flaked almonds, chopped and toasted	2 oz	½ cup
225 g	Cream or cottage cheese	8 oz	1 cup
1	Lemon, juice of	1	1
1 tbsp	Dry white wine	1 tbsp	1 tbsp
2 tbsp	Mayonnaise	2 tbsp	2 tbsp
1 tbsp	Double cream	1 tbsp	1 tbsp
	Tabasco and Worcestershire sauces		
1	Lettuce, washed and dried	1	1

1. Stir the almonds into the cheese and form the mixture into small balls. Chill for 1 hour.
2. To make the sauce, combine the wine, mayonnaise and cream with a dash of each sauce. Season to taste.
3. Shred the outer lettuce leaves and place in a serving dish with the quartered heart on top.
4. Peel, core and halve the pears, and brush with lemon juice to prevent discolouration.
5. Pile the cheese balls on to the pear halves on the shredded lettuce. Pour the sauce over.

THE CARNE CROSS *in Gloucester Cathedral was carved by Lt. Col. Carne, V.C. of the First Batallion, Gloucester Regiment, whilst in solitary confinement as a Korean prisoner of war. It was subsequently used at the camp religious services.*

STILTON AND WALNUT PATE   *Serves 4*

The Tara Hotel at Gloucester serves this with toasted brown bread.

Metric		lb/oz	U.S.A.
125 g	Cottage cheese	4 oz	½ cup
30 g	Butter	1 oz	2 tbsp
45 g	Stilton cheese	1½ oz	⅓ cup
	Brown breadcrumbs, dried		
1 tsp	Dijon mustard	1 tsp	1 tsp
45 g	Ground walnuts	1½ oz	⅓ cup
½ tsp	Caraway seeds or chopped parsley	½ tsp	½ tsp

1. Blend the cottage cheese, butter and Stilton until creamy.
2. Add the breadcrumbs and mustard. Fold in the walnuts and caraway seeds or parsley. Season to taste.
3. Divide the pâté between individual ramekin dishes, or place each portion on a lettuce leaf on a serving dish.

Main Dishes

GLOUCESTERSHIRE HAM BAKE   *Serves 6*

Enjoy this Cathedral Refectory speciality in your own home.

Metric		lb/oz	U.S.A.
	500 g (1 lb) Cooked ham, cubed		
1	*Large onion, chopped*	1	1
60 g	*Butter*	2 oz	¼ cup
90 g	*Flour*	3 oz	¾ cup
300 ml	*Milk*	½ pt	1 cup
500 g	*Potato, cooked and diced*	1 lb	4 cups
125 g	*Peas, cooked*	4 oz	1 cup
125 g	*Mushrooms, sliced*	4 oz	1 cup
225 g	*Cheddar cheese, grated*	8 oz	2 cups

1. Set the oven to 190°C, 375°F, Gas Mark 5.
2. Simmer the onion in salted water for 15 minutes.
3. Meanwhile, melt the butter in a saucepan over a gentle heat. Stir in the flour for 2-3 minutes to make a smooth roux. Add the milk gradually, stirring continuously.
4. Gradually stir in the onion and ½ pint liquor from the onion.
5. Gradually add three-quarters of the cheese, stirring until smooth. Season to taste and remove from the heat.
6. Put all the remaining ingredients (except cheese) into an ovenproof casserole. Pour over the sauce, sprinkle on the cheese, and bake until heated through and golden brown, about 15-20 minutes.

GLOUCESTER'S OLD SPOT *was once common, but is now a rare breed. It is also known as the 'orchard pig' because it used to be kept in apple orchards. No part of the pig was wasted, every bit used in dishes like faggots, black pudding and brawn, and to make lard.*

TROPICAL PORK   *Serves 4*

This rich, special occasion dish comes from the Black Tulip in Cheltenham. Go on, treat yourself!

Metric		lb/oz	U.S.A.
	700 g (1½ lb) Pork fillet, cut into 60 g (2 oz) rounds		
250 g	Tomatoes	8 oz	1 cup
125 g	Desiccated coconut	4 oz	1 cup
60 g	Butter	2 oz	¼ cup
125 g	Fresh pineapple, diced	4 oz	¾ cup
60 g	Onion, diced	2 oz	½ cup
30 g	Curry powder	1 oz	¼ cup
90 ml	Dark rum	4 fl. oz	½ cup
600 ml	Whipping cream	1 pt	2½ cups
3 tbsp	Chopped parsley	3 tbsp	¼ cup

1. Plunge the tomatoes into boiling water, then skin, de-seed and chop roughly.
2. Coat the pork in coconut and fry lightly on both sides in the butter. Remove and keep warm.
3. Put the tomato, pineapple, onion and curry powder in the pan and fry lightly until the onion is soft and transparent. Return the pork to the pan.
4. Pour the rum into the pan and flambé. While it is still flaming, add the cream and parsley. Season to taste, and simmer very gently to reduce to a thick sauce.
5. Transfer to a warmed dish and serve immediately.

Editor's Note: This sauce is very rich and generous in quantity. You could cut the amount of rum and cream and still enjoy this dish.

'A man is what he eats.'   LUDWIG FEUERBACH

PORK ESCALOPES IN MANGO SAUCE   *Serves 4*

Sweet, spicy, colourful and mouthwatering – who could ask for anything more? Try it at Below Stairs, Cheltenham.

Metric		lb/oz	U.S.A.
	500g (1 lb) Pork fillet, trimmed of fat		
2 tbsp	Seasoned flour	2 tbsp	2 tbsp
60 g	Butter	2 oz	¼ cup
1 tbsp	Oil	1 tbsp	1 tbsp
2 tbsp	Calvados	2 tbsp	2 tbsp
3	Small peppers, 1 green, 1 red, 1 yellow, de-seeded and finely sliced	3	3
1	Onion, finely chopped	1	1
300 ml	Chicken stock	½ pt	1 cup
2 tbsp	Mango chutney	2 tbsp	2 tbsp
1 tbsp	Cornflour	1 tbsp	1 tbsp
	Lettuce and fresh mango to garnish		

1. Slice the pork, place between sheets of polythene and beat out extremely thinly with a meat hammer or rolling pin. Coat with seasoned flour.
2. Heat half the butter in a large frying pan with the oil. Fry the escalopes over a high heat for 1 minute on each side to brown them. Pour in the Calvados and flambé. When the flames die down, remove the meat and keep warm.
3. To make the sauce, melt the remaining butter in the same pan and gently fry the peppers and onion until soft but not browned. Gradually stir in the stock, then add the chutney. Slake the cornflour with a little cold water and stir in enough to make a fairly thick sauce.
4. Return the escalopes to the pan and simmer in the sauce for a minute or two to heat through. Transfer to a serving dish, garnish with slices of mango and quarters of lettuce heart.

'It is said that the effect of eating too much lettuce is soporific.'
The Tale of The Flopsy Bunnies
BEATRIX POTTER, 1866-1943

PORK FILLET EN CROUTE WITH PRUNE COMPOTE *Serves 4*

You'll have to make the compôte in advance for this dish from the Gentle Gardener, Tetbury, but it's well worth the effort.

Metric		lb/oz	U.S.A.
	500 g (1 lb) Lean pork fillet		
60 g	Butter	2 oz	¼ cup
1 tbsp	Onions, finely chopped	1 tbsp	1 tbsp
85 g	Mushrooms, chopped	3 oz	1 cup
2 tbsp	Chopped parsley	2 tbsp	3 tbsp
60 g	Fresh breadcrumbs	2 oz	1 cup
1	Egg yolk	1	1
225 g	Puff pastry	8 oz	½ lb
	Prune compôte, made in advance (see p. 74)		

1. Melt the butter in a pan and sauté the pork until browned and sealed. Remove and leave to cool.
2. Meanwhile, fry the onion in the butter until soft. Add the mushrooms and fry for a further 5 minutes. Mix in the parsley, breadcrumbs and egg yolk and season well.
3. Split the pork lengthways to make a pocket. Fill with the stuffing.
4. Set the oven to 210°C, 425°F, Gas Mark 7.
5. Roll the pastry out to 6 mm (¼") thick. Wrap the fillet in it, damping and sealing the edges. Place on a baking sheet with the fold underneath. Bake for 15 minutes, then reduce the heat to 190°C, 375°F, Gas Mark 5, and bake for a further 10-15 minutes.
6. Cut into slices and offer the prune compôte, hot or cold as preferred, separately.

FILLET OF BEEF ESTCOURT GRANGE *Serves 2*

A lovely contribution from the equally delightful Snooty Fox at Tetbury.

Metric		lb/oz	U.S.A.
	500 g (1 lb) Fillet steak		
60 g	Flour	2 oz	½ cup
60 g	Butter	2 oz	½ cup
3 tbsp	Port	3 tbsp	¼ cup
85 ml	Single cream	3 fl. oz	⅓ cup
1	Peach, stoned and sliced	1	1
	Chopped parsley to garnish		

1. Cut the steak into 12 slices, and flatten lightly with a meat hammer or rolling pin and coat in the flour.
2. Melt the butter in a pan and fry the steaks to taste, turning once. Remove and keep warm.

3. Pour the port into the pan and flambé. When slightly reduced, stir in the cream and simmer very gently to make a thick sauce. Season to taste.
4. To serve, arrange five slices of meat around each plate with the sixth one in the centre. Cover this one with peach slices. Coat the meat with the sauce and garnish with parsley.

THE SEVERN BORE

One of the most impressive natural phenomena to be seen in England, the bore is a huge wall of water spanning the river. Travelling at speeds of up to 10 m.p.h. and reaching up to 6' high, the bore is caused by a very high tide being forced up the estuary. The bore is at its highest every full moon.

FILLET OF BEEF IN STILTON SAUCE   *Serves 2*

Visit Wotton-under-Edge to sample this great dish at the Swan Hotel.

Metric		lb/oz	U.S.A.
	2 × 225 g (8 oz) Fillet steaks		
2	*Garlic cloves*	2	2
60 g	*Butter*	2 oz	¼ cup
30 g	*Onion, chopped*	1 oz	¼ cup
15 g	*Bacon, chopped*	½ oz	1 tbsp
60 g	*Mushrooms, sliced*	2 oz	½ cup
150 ml	*Milk*	¼ pt	½ cup
60 g	*Stilton, crumbled*	2 oz	½ cup
150 ml	*Double cream*	¼ pt	½ cup

1. Flatten the steaks to about 2.5 cm (1") thickness with a meat hammer or rolling pin. Season with salt and freshly ground black pepper, and rub with half the garlic.
2. Melt half the butter in a pan and fry the steaks for about 1 minute on each side to seal them. Remove and keep warm.
3. Add the remaining butter to the pan and fry the onion and bacon for 3-4 minutes. Add the mushrooms, the remaining garlic, milk and Stilton. Allow to boil, stirring until the Stilton has been fully absorbed.
4. Reduce the heat, add the cream and season to taste. Return the steaks to the sauce and simmer until cooked as desired.

THE NEW INN, NORTHGATE STREET

Built by the Abbey to shelter pilgrims visiting the Gloucester Cathedral shrine of Edward II, the New Inn dates from about 1457. There is an interesting 15th century carving on the corner of the alleyway, and the courtyard and gallery beyond are considered to among the finest of their kind.

VOL-AU-VENTS DE BOEUF BOURGEOISES   *Serves 2*

A treat to look forward to at the Hotel de la Bere, Southam.

Metric		lb/oz	U.S.A.
	275g (10oz) Fillet steak, trimmed of all fat		
2 tbsp	Seasoned flour	2 tbsp	2 tbsp
275 g	Puff pastry	10 oz	10 oz
1	Egg, beaten	1	1
60 g	Butter	2 oz	¼ cup
	Oil for frying		
3	Shallots, finely chopped	3	3
1	Garlic clove, crushed	1	1
125 ml	Red wine	4 fl. oz	½ cup
½	Bay leaf	½	½
150 ml	Beef stock	¼ pt	½ cup
1 tbsp	Tomato purée	1 tbsp	1 tbsp
6	Small onions, peeled	6	6
2	Rashers of back bacon	2	2
125 g	Button mushrooms	4 oz	2 cups
60 g	Margarine	2 oz	¼ cup
60 g	Flour	2 oz	½ cup
	Parsley to garnish		

1. Set the oven to 210°C, 425°F, Gas Mark 7.
2. First make the vol-au-vent cases. Roll the pastry out to ½ cm (¼") thick, and cut into two large oval shapes. Score with a knife, but don't cut right through, 1 cm (½ in) inside the edge. Brush with beaten egg and leave for 20 minutes.
3. Bake the cases for about 20 minutes until well risen and golden brown. Lift off the lids, removing any soft filling, and keep warm in the bottom of the oven. Turn the oven down to 180°C, 350°F, Gas Mark 4.
4. While the vol-au-vents are cooking, heat the butter and 1 tbsp of oil in a shallow casserole. Add the shallots and garlic, cook until soft and remove from the heat.
5. Cut the meat into 1 cm × 1 cm × 5 cm (½" × ½" × 2") strips, and roll in seasoned flour. Add to the pan and fry quickly to seal. Pour in the wine, add the bay leaf and simmer rapidly for 2 minutes to reduce, then add the stock and tomato purée. Cover and bake for about 25 minutes or until tender.
6. Meanwhile, blanch the small onions briefly in boiling water, then braise in a little oil until cooked through. Cut the bacon into slices and fry lightly. Gently poach the mushrooms.
7. Melt the margarine in a small pan, stir in the flour and cook gently for 1-2 minutes to make a pale roux.
8. Remove the meat from the casserole and keep warm. Heat the liquid and whisk in the roux a little at a time to make a thick sauce.
9. Put the meat back into the sauce and add the onions, bacon and mushrooms.
10. Fill each vol-au-vent case with the mixture, replace the lids and serve at once garnished with parsley.

FAITH, HOPE AND CHARITY *were famous wartime 'Gladiators'. Both Gladiators, and later thousands of 'Hurricanes', were manufactured at the heavily camouflaged Gloucester factory.*

VEAL SWEETBREADS IN CHEESE SAUCE   *Serves 4-6*

The Greenway Hotel at Shurdington have created this delicacy.

Metric		lb/oz	U.S.A.
	700 g (1½ lb) Veal sweetbreads		
30 g	*Butter*	1 oz	2 tbsp
250 g	*Mushrooms, finely chopped*	8 oz	2 cups
1	*Onion, finely chopped*	1	½ cup
1	*Garlic clove, crushed*	1	1
2 tbsp	*Chopped parsley to garnish*	2 tbsp	2 tbsp
	For the cheese sauce:		
30 g	*Butter*	1 oz	2 tbsp
30 g	*Plain flour*	1 oz	¼ cup
600 ml	*Milk, warmed*	1 pt	2½ cups
175 g	*Cheddar cheese, grated*	6 oz	1½ cups
150 ml	*Double cream*	¼ pt	½ cup

1. Wash the sweetbreads thoroughly. Poach in gently simmering, salted water for 10-20 minutes, until firm. Drain and cool.
2. Melt the butter in a saucepan and fry the mushrooms, onions, and garlic until cooked.
3. To make the sauce, melt the butter in a small pan, add the flour and cook gently, until grainy. Cool slightly. Gradually add the milk, stirring. Cook for 20 minutes.
4. Add the cheese and cream. Stir until smooth and pass through a fine sieve into a bowl set over a pan of boiling water.
5. Remove all skin and gristle from the sweetbreads and cut them into 12-18 slices. Set the grill to high.
6. Ladle the sauce into a shallow heatproof serving dish. Arrange the sweetbread slices neatly on top and spoon the mushroom mixture over them. Grill until the sauce turns golden, and serve garnished with the parsley.

THE GLOSTER AIRCRAFT COMPANY, *formed in 1915, pioneered the 'Gloster Whittle' and the world's first jet fighter, the 'Gloster Meteor'. In the Second World War, the three intrepid 'Sea Gladiators' (above) tenaciously defended Malta.*

TOURNEDOS OF VEAL WITH NOILLY PRAT SAUCE *Serves 6*

If you are visiting the Corse Lawn House Hotel, let's hope that this light and creamy offering is on the menu – you won't regret choosing it.

Metric		*lb/oz*	*U.S.A.*
	2 Whole veal fillets, trimmed of fat and cut into 6 tournedos		
	Bacon, optional – see method		
60 g	Clarified butter*	2 oz	¼ cup
90 ml	Veal stock	3½ fl. oz	½ cup
90 ml	Noilly Prat	3½ fl. oz	½ cup
	For the mushroom mousseline:		
125 g	Mushrooms, chopped	4 oz	1 cup
30 g	Butter	1 oz	2 tbsp
3	Egg whites	3	3
90 ml	Double cream	3½ fl. oz	½ cup

* To clarify butter, melt over a gentle heat. Remove and set aside until the milky solids settle. Skim the clarified butter from the top and transfer to a bowl. Cover and refrigerate until needed.

1. To make the mousseline, fry the mushrooms in the butter, season and allow to cool. Place in a blender with the egg whites and blend until smooth. Pour into a bowl set over crushed ice and stir in the cream.
2. Butter a large, shallow baking dish, pour in the mixture and cover with foil. Stand the dish in a roasting tin half full of hot water and simmer on the stove for 15 minutes.
3. Meanwhile, fry the tournedos slowly in the clarified butter, turning occasionally, for 10-15 minutes or until cooked through. (If preferred, they can be wrapped in bacon to retain maximum flavour.) Remove from the pan and keep warm.
4. Pour the veal stock into the pan, add the Noilly Prat and reduce to a syrupy consistency. Season to taste.
5. Pour the sauce on to 6 warmed plates and place a tournedo on to each. Cut the mousseline into rounds with a biscuit cutter and place on top of the tournedos.

GLOUCESTER DOCKS

One of Gloucester's most famous features is its docks, familiar to millions through the period television series 'The Onedin Line'. The docks and warehouses cover an area of 14 acres, with over a thousand feet of quays, and Continental cargo ships are still regular visitors.

It was because it was at the lowest crossing point of the River Severn that the Romans established their fortress of Glevum here. But it was after Elizabeth I granted it port status in 1580 that trade really boomed — so much so that local merchants had to build a canal linking the port with the Severn estuary.

SPICED LAMB

Serves 6

Great to serve on cold winter evenings, this dish won't spoil if you are late getting home or if your guests are delayed. The recipe comes from Graham Ruddock of Tasters Wine Bar in Gloucester.

Metric		lb/oz	U.S.A.
	1 kg (2 lb) Lean lamb, trimmed and cubed		
	Oil for frying		
2	*Onions, chopped*	2	1 cup
125 ml	*Red wine*	4 fl. oz	½ cup
400 g	*Tomatoes, can of*	14 oz	14 oz
2	*Garlic cloves, crushed*	2	2
1 tsp	*Turmeric*	1 tsp	1 tsp
½ tsp	*Ground ginger*	½ tsp	½ tsp
½ tsp	*Mild chilli powder*	½ tsp	½ tsp
125 g	*Seedless raisins*	4 oz	⅔ cup

1. Fry the meat in a little oil in a casserole until lightly browned. Season with salt and freshly ground black pepper.
2. Remove the meat and fry the onion until softened.
3. Return the meat to the casserole and stir in all the remaining ingredients. Bring to the boil, then simmer very gently for 1½ hours.

GEORGE WHITFIELD, *the famous American Evangelist, was born at the Bell Hotel, Gloucester, on 16th December 1714. He was ordained on 20th June, 1736, and preached his first sermon in St. Mary de Crypt six days later.*

TURN AGAIN WHITTINGTON, LORD OF PAUNTLEY COURT

Dick Whittington was born at Pauntley in 1358 — not the poor kitchen boy of legend, but the third son of Sir William Whittington. Neither did he graduate from the garret to marry his master's daughter, but espoused the daughter of a neighbouring country gentleman. But whilst a child, his father was outlawed for marrying a Berkeley widow without a royal sanction. Dick was apprenticed to a mercer, and quickly progressed to become the most famous merchant of his day. Four times Lord Mayor of London, he devoted much of his later years to public service, repairing St. Bartholomew's Hospital in London and rebuilding Newgate prison. The Chapel of St. George in Pauntley Village Church is thought to be a gift from him, and his coat of arms can be seen in the tower window.

BISHOP HOOPER'S LODGING

*This medieval, half-timbered building stands in Westgate Street, and is believed to be where Bishop John Hooper spent his last night. The Lutheran bishop, a victim of Mary Tudor's religious persecutions, was burnt at the stake in 1555 in St. Mary's Square, where a monument was erected to him in 1862. Today, the lodging is home for the **Gloucester Folk Museum**, whose exhibits are a testimony to the crafts and skills and the area's agricultural and industrial past.*

LAMB IN ORANGE AND GINGER   *Serves 4*

Here's how to make everyday ingredients into something special. The recipe comes from the kitchens of Below Stairs, Cheltenham.

Metric		lb/oz	U.S.A.
	4 Chump chops		
2 tbsp	Seasoned flour	2 tbsp	2 tbsp
	Olive oil for frying		
	Butter for frying		
200 ml	Orange juice, can of	⅓ pt	¾ cup
6	Preserved ginger, pieces	6	6
1	Orange, sliced	1	1
1	Bunch of watercress to garnish	1	1

1. Set the oven to 170°C, 325°F, Gas Mark 3.
2. Trim the chops of all fat, and coat in seasoned flour. Fry briefly in hot oil to seal in the juices.
3. Place the chops in a casserole. Pour in the orange juice diluted with half a can of water. Chop and add the ginger. Bring to the boil, cover and put in the oven for an hour.
4. Just before serving, peel the orange, slice it thinly and fry in a little butter. Garnish each chop with orange slices and a sprig of watercress.

Painswick

*"Mincing Hampton and Painswick Proud
Beggarly Bisley and Strutting Stroud!"*

Situated on a high spur between two valleys, this ageless town has earned the name 'Queen of the Cotswolds'. Once at the heart of the clothing industry, its homes and streets still retain an atmosphere of times long gone.

THE PUPPY DOG PIE LEGEND (*see page 45*) *draws on the ancient rivalry between Painswick and Stroud. A Painswick host was reputed to have served his Stroudian guests dog meat, and from then on Painswickians were nicknamed 'Bow wows' or 'Doggies' and Stroudians 'Gothamites' or 'Simpletons'. Stick fighting was frequent, as was verbal touting.*

*"What are little boys made of?
Frogs and snails
And puppy-dogs' tails,
That's what little boys are made of."*

GOING WALKABOUT

The streets and lanes of Painswick are well worth exploring.
Look out for names which date back to the heyday of the wool
industry, such as Silk Mill Street and Lower Washwell Lane.

The churchyard, with its extraordinary collection of merchants'
tombs, is also known for its impressive number of clipped yew
trees. Some say only 99 will survive because the devil always
takes the hundredth! They are, indeed, difficult to count, but
there were 104 planted some 270 years ago, each one ten
paces from its neighbour.

Each September the church holds a 'clipping' ceremony
believed to date back to medieval times when dogs were
sacrificed to the patron saint of shepherds. Singing hymns, the
parishoners circle the church hand-in-hand. As a substitute for
'puppy dog pie', which was traditionally baked on the feast day,
the village children are given cakes to eat!

During the Civil War, Parliamentary troops took refuge in the
15th century church, and its walls are still marked by the flames
that forced them to surrender.

On a happier note, there is a cluster of houses on a forested hill
near to Painswick called 'Paradise'. It is thought to have been
given the name by Charles I. The local inn, once 'The Plough',
has been more fittingly re-named, 'The Adam and Eve'.

TAKING THE TOMB TRAIL

There are so many fascinating and unusual old tombs in Painswick Churchyard — like the one shown here — that a guide has been produced! Most belonged to rich 18th century clothing merchants.

STUFFED CHICKEN BREASTS WITH CHAMBERY   Serves 4

Visitors dining at the Cleeveway House Restaurant at Bishop's Cleeve can enjoy this dish, and it is certainly worth making the effort to re-create it in your own home.

Metric		lb/oz	U.S.A.
	4 Chicken suprêmes, skinned		
125 g	*Butter*	4 oz	½ cup
1	*Large onion, finely chopped*	1	1
125 g	*Spinach, trimmed*	4 oz	¼ lb
1	*Lime or small lemon*	1	1
60 g	*Blanched almonds, chopped*	2 oz	⅔ cup
¼ bottle	*Chambèry*	¼ bottle	¼ bottle
125 ml	*Double cream*	¼ pt	½ cup
	Chopped parsley to garnish		

1. To make the stuffing, melt half the butter in a frying pan, add the onion and cook until soft but not browned. Add the spinach and grated lime rind, then season to taste and cook until soft.
2. Add the lime juice and almonds. Stir, season to taste, and leave to cool.
3. Put the stuffing into a liquidizer or food processor for a few seconds. Make a pocket in each chicken breast, divide the stuffing between them and season.
4. Heat the remaining butter and fry the suprêmes briefly to brown on both sides. Pour in the Chambèry, cover and cook gently for 10 minutes.
5. Transfer the chicken to a pre-heated dish and keep warm. Add the cream to the pan juices and simmer gently to make a thick sauce. Pour the sauce over the chicken and sprinkle with parsley.

A ROMANTIC TOUCH
Look out for this sign as you wander through Painswick.

"What are little girls made of?
Sugar and spice
And all things nice
That's what little girls are made of."

"His wit is as thick as Tewkesbury mustard."

Sir John Falstaff
Henry IV, Part 2
WILLIAM SHAKESPEARE, 1564-1616

BREASTS OF CHICKEN WITH HAWAIIAN SAUCE   *Serves 4*

No need to wear a grass skirt when you enjoy this dish at the Bell Hotel in Tewkesbury, who gave us the recipe. Humble chicken is given a magic touch when coated with their delicious sauce combining the flavours and textures of pineapple, prawns and cream.

Metric		lb/oz	U.S.A.
	4 Chicken suprêmes		
85 g	*Butter*	3 oz	⅓ cup
1 tbsp	*Seasoned flour*	1 tbsp	1 tbsp
	For the Hawaiian sauce:		
1	*Small onion, finely chopped*	1	1
4	*Pineapple slices, crushed*	4	4
450 ml	*Dry white wine*	¾ pt	1½ cups
350 g	*Peeled prawns*	12 oz	2 cups
300 ml	*Double cream*	½ pt	1 cup

1. Heat two-thirds of the butter in a pan. Lightly coat the breasts with seasoned flour and fry very gently for 7-9 minutes on each side, until cooked but not browned. Transfer to a serving dish and keep warm.
2. To make the sauce, put the remaining butter in the pan, add the onion and fry gently until soft and transparent. Season, then add the pineapple and cook for 2-3 minutes.
3. Pour in the wine and simmer for 5 minutes, then add the prawns and cream. Cook very gently until the sauce reduces and thickens and pour it over the chicken.

PAINSWICK BEACON at 928' high offers panoramic views over the Black Mountains, the Brecon Beacons and the Malvern Hills.

SLIMBRIDGE WILDFOWL TRUST *on the marshlands of the Severn estuary was founded in 1946 by Sir Peter Scott, and contains the world's finest collection of wildfowl. A sanctuary for a colourful bird population from all over the world, it provides a safe breeding ground for every kind of fowl from Andean flamingoes to whooper swans to Australian pink-eared ducks! Bird-lovers are encouraged to 'adopt a duck' or 'sponsor a swan'.*

STUFFED CHICKEN BREASTS IN CURRY SAUCE   *Serves 4*

In this regal offering from the Gentle Gardener at Tetbury an apricot stuffing and creamy curry sauce transform an everyday ingredient into a dish fit for a prince.

Metric		lb/oz	U.S.A.
	4 Chicken breast and wing joints		
1	Small onion, chopped	1	1
75 g	Dried apricots, soaked and finely chopped	3 oz	½ cup
300 ml	Dry white wine	½ pt	1 cup
85 g	Bulgar wheat* or brown rice	3 oz	⅓ cup
	Runny honey to glaze		
	For the sauce:		
150 ml	Double cream	¼ pt	½ cup
2 tsp	Curry powder	2 tsp	2 tsp
1 tsp	Ground ginger	1 tsp	1 tsp
2 tbsp	Mango chutney	2 tbsp	2 tbsp
1 tbsp	Apricot jam	1 tbsp	1 tbsp

1. Remove the second wing joint and remains of the carcass from the chicken pieces but leave the skin on. This leaves an almost completely boneless chicken breast. The fillet on the underside makes the beginning of a slit; deepen this to take the stuffing.
2. Simmer the onion in 300 ml (½ pt, 1 cup) of water with chicken bones or a stock cube to make stock.
3. Simmer the apricots in the wine for about 10 minutes until tender.
4. Simmer the bulgar or rice in the stock and any wine not absorbed by the apricots for 45 minutes.
5. Set the oven to 190°C, 375°F, Gas Mark 5. Grease a baking tray. Combine the bulgar or rice with the apricots and season well. Make a slit in each chicken breast and pack with stuffing. Secure with wooden cocktail sticks, place on a baking sheet, and brush with honey. Roast for 20 minutes.
6. Meanwhile, liquidize all the sauce ingredients into a smooth cream. To serve, heat gently and pour over the cooked chicken breasts, first removing the cocktail sticks. Garnish with slices of mango from the chutney jar.

* Bulgar wheat can be obtained at most health food shops – Editor.

GROVEWOOD CHICKEN

Serves 2

A mouthwatering almond and lemon butter is the secret of this crispy coated chicken treat from the Snooty Fox, Tetbury.

Metric		lb/oz	U.S.A.
	2 Chicken suprêmes		
225 g	*Butter, softened*	8 oz	1 cup
225 g	*Nibbed almonds*	8 oz	2½ cups
1	*Lemon*	1	1
2 tbsp	*Seasoned flour*	2 tbsp	2 tbsp
4 tbsp	*Milk*	4 tbsp	⅓ cup
150 g	*Mushrooms, poached*	5 oz	1 cup
300 ml	*Velouté sauce (see p. 75)*	½ pt	1 cup
	Parsley sprigs to garnish		

1. Mix half the butter with a quarter of the almonds and the juice of half the lemon. Refrigerate. Cut the remaining lemon half into segments and reserve.
2. Make a 'pocket' in each breast, and fill with almond butter.
3. Roll the parcels in seasoned flour, dip in milk and coat with the reserved almonds. Fry in the remaining butter until golden brown.
4. Add the chopped mushrooms to the velouté, with a little cream if liked. Coat the parcels, and garnish with parsley and lemon segments.

PRINKNASH ABBEY

Two and a half miles from Painswick is the religious community of Prinknash Abbey — pronounced 'Prinage'. The old Abbey is situated in a 400-year old manor house, providing a sharp contrast to the new Abbey consecrated in 1972. In the past the old house has been an abbey, mill, country house and hunting lodge, but the monastic communal life of the Benedictines now goes on undisturbed, and Prinknash pottery is sent all over the world.

A bird park in the grounds contains fishponds built by monks before the Reformation. It boasts many waterfowl, including pheasants, peacocks, swans and geese.

Tewkesbury

At the crossing point of the Rivers Severn and Avon stands Tewkesbury, one of England's pre-eminent historical towns. The town grew up around its magnificent Norman Abbey on the banks of the Avon, and today boasts some of the finest half-timbered buildings in the country. For example, **The Black Bear**, one of Gloucestershire's oldest inns, dates from 1308. Another inn, **The Hop Pole**, was chosen by **Dickens** as a stopping-off place for Mr. Pickwick, who dined so well that he fell asleep for the next 30 miles!

> *"At the Hop Pole Tewkesbury they stopped to dine, upon which the occasion there was more bottled ale, with some Madeira and Port besides."*

In Shakespeare's day, Tewkesbury was renowned for its mustard. One of Falstaff's witticisms in Henry IV, Part 2 is: "His wit is as thick as Tewkesbury mustard".

A famous Tewkesbury resident was the novelist **John Moore**. 'Elmbury', part of 'The Brensham Trilogy', was set in and around Tewkesbury. A museum named in his honour houses many country exhibits.

The Battle of Tewkesbury

From Lincoln Lane, the famous 'Bloody Meadow' where the Battle of Tewkesbury took place on the 4th May, 1417, can be seen. This was the decisive and most bloody battle of the Wars of the Roses, when the army of Queen Margaret, wife of Henry VI, was defeated by King Edward IV, thereby losing the cause of the House of Lancaster. Many who fled after the battle to seek refuge at the Abbey altar were slaughtered there.

The Civil War

Tewkesbury also played a prominent part in the Civil War, and on one occasion received a request from Charles I for every spade, mattock and shovel in the town, to aid him in his seige of Gloucester.

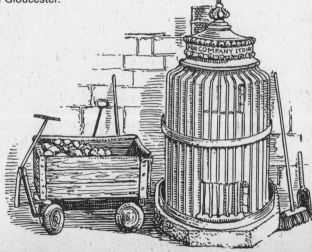

TEWKESBURY ABBEY

Used for religious worship since the middle of the 7th century, when a monk called Theoc built a cell here, Tewkesbury Abbey is sited on the banks of the River Avon. Theoc's cell was replaced by a Benedictine monastery of which there is now no trace, and the present Abbey was begun by William the Conqueror's cousin, Robert FitzHamon in 1092. The Abbey was ultimately consecrated in 1121 and was fortunately saved during Henry VIII's dissolution of the monasteries by the Tewkesbury townsfolk who bought it for £453. Today it is the second largest parish church in England, and inside is the longest medieval altar in England, made of Purbeck marble.

ANCIENT AND MODERN

Have you ever wondered how you would set about heating a church? The Victorians installed this amazing heating system in Tewkesbury Abbey. No doubt an innovation in its time, this fine old giant still pumps out heat when fed with coal from the equally splendid trolley alongside!

52

BARGE BOUILLABAISE

Serves 4-6

Whenever it's on the menu at the Barge Semington Arts Centre in Gloucester Docks, this 'sailors' treat' is universally popular.

Metric		lb/oz	U.S.A.
	1 kg (2 lb) Mixed fish: whiting, mackerel, rock salmon, squid, red mullet, large prawns, crab		
2	Large onions, sliced	2	2
1	Head of fennel, chopped	1	1
2	Celery sticks, chopped	2	2
150 ml	Olive oil (preferably virgin)	¼ pt	½ cup
225 g	Ripe tomatoes, skinned	8 oz	1 cup
2	Garlic cloves, crushed	2	2
1	Bay leaf	1	1
½ tsp	Thyme	½ tsp	½ tsp
½ tsp	Fennel seed	½ tsp	½ tsp
1	Orange, grated rind of	1	1
1	Bunch of fresh parsley	1	1
1	Saffron, pinch of	1	1
2	Egg yolks, beaten	2	2
150 ml	Double cream	¼ pt	½ cup
60 g	Parmesan cheese, grated	2 oz	½ cup

1. Clean and skin the fish and cut it into fairly thick pieces. Remove shellfish from shells.
2. Fry the onion, fennel and celery in the oil until soft but not browned. Add the tomatoes, garlic, bay leaf, thyme, fennel seeds, orange rind and most of the parsley (reserving some sprigs to garnish).
3. Layer the firm fleshed fish (mackerel, rock salmon, squid) over the vegetables. Dissolve the saffron in a little water and pour over. Just cover with water, bring to the boil and simmer for 8 minutes.
4. Add the softer fish (whiting, red mullet, shellfish) and cook for a further 5 minutes or until cooked but still firm.
5. Season just before serving, then stir in the egg yolks. Pour into bowls and garnish with a swirl of cream, a sprinkling of Parmesan and a sprig of parsley.

"Where you eat is sacred." MEL BROOKS

(American Film Director)

BEAUCHAMP CHAPEL VAULTING

The chapel in Tewkesbury Abbey, built by Isobella Despenser for her husband Richard Beauchamp, took 16 years to build and was completed in 1438. It is a beautiful example of late Gothic architecture featuring some of the earliest examples of fan vaulting.

'Thou deboshed fish thou' The Tempest, Act 3, Scene 2
WILLIAM SHAKESPEARE, 1564-1616

THESE SALMON AND ELVER FISHING IMPLEMENTS *can all
be seen in the Gloucester Folk Museum.
Severn eels were undoubtedly deboshed when caught on this
vicious-looking eelspear (1). Although forbidden in 1532, eel-
spearing continued to be practised until 1911.
The saying goes 'as slippery as an eel', which is why the eel
wheel (2) was designed with wooden staves inside to prevent
the eel escaping. The Molly knocker (3) was used for stunning
the fish on the head. A salmon putcher (4) has three sections —
the kype, butt and forewheel. It is said that the close woven
putcher will even catch a shrimp.*

(1) (2) (3)

*An elver fisherman uses a curiously-shaped net (5). Elvers were
fished on the spring tides, so as well as his tealing sticks, bucket
and sack, he would also carry a lamp. Huge shoals can be
found all along the Estuary, and there are annual elver-eating
contests at Frampton-on-Severn and Epney. The world record
was claimed by a Frampton farmer in 1975 when he downed
1,300 elvers in 44 seconds!*

SEAFOOD RAGOUT   *Serves 4*

The recipe for this colourful seafood medley comes from the
Chef of the Painswick Hotel.

Metric		lb/oz	U.S.A.
4	*Scallops*	4	4
4	*Small fillets of monkfish*	4	4
175 g	*Sea bass fillet*	6 oz	6 oz
175 g	*Lemon sole fillet*	6 oz	6 oz
125 g	*Butter*	4 oz	½ cup
125 g	*Button mushrooms, sliced*	4 oz	1 cup
3 tbsp	*Dry vermouth*	3 tbsp	¼ cup
600 ml	*Fish stock (see page 75)*	1 pt	2½ cups
	Saffron, pinch of		
150 ml	*Double cream*	¼ pt	½ cup

1. Cut all the fish fillets into 4 pieces and season.
2. Melt a quarter of the butter in a pan, add the fish and cook over a high heat, stirring continuously for 2-3 minutes. Add the scallops and cook for a further minute. Remove and keep warm.
3. Add a little more butter to the pan and fry the mushrooms gently for 2 minutes. Pour in the vermouth and stir to deglaze the pan. Add the stock and saffron. Remove the mushrooms and put on one side with the fish.
4. Boil up the fish stock to reduce it by two-thirds. Add the cream and simmer gently until reduced by half. Whisk in the remaining butter to give the sauce a good shine.
5. Add the fish and mushrooms and heat through. Season to taste and serve with rice.

(4) (5)

FILLETS OF TURBOT IN NOILLY PRAT SAUCE Serves 4

Here's how Chef Bennett of the Greenway Hotel, Shurdington, gives the humble turbot royal treatment.

Metric		lb/oz	U.S.A.
	700 g (1½ lb) Turbot fillet		
2 tbsp	Seasoned flour	2 tbsp	2 tbsp
125 g	Butter	4 oz	½ cup
2 tbsp	Noilly Prat	2 tbsp	2 tbsp
600 ml	Fish stock made from turbot bones (see page 75)	1 pt	2½ cups
1	Lemon, juice of	1	1
2 tbsp	Chopped chives	2 tbsp	2 tbsp

1. Slice the turbot fillets on the slant into even pieces. Toss very lightly in seasoned flour and pat off the excess.
2. Melt half the butter in a frying pan and fry the fillets quickly, turning once, until golden brown. Remove from the pan, place in a shallow serving dish and keep warm.
3. Stir the Noilly Prat into the pan juices and simmer until reduced by half. Add the fish stock and boil until syrupy. Dice the remaining butter and stir into the sauce until smooth. Add the lemon juice and season to taste.
4. Spoon the sauce over the fish, and sprinkle the chives on top. Serve at once.

TEWKESBURY MILL   *(see overleaf)*

DANGER
SLUICES
KEEP CLEAR

TEWKESBURY MILL *(see previous page)*

The foundations of this imposing building were laid in 1190 as part of the water supply system built by early Benedictine monks. Along the millpond banks is a row of half-timbered cottages, formerly the property of the Abbey and now called Millbank.

The Mill is famous for its prominent part in the Victorian melodrama 'John Halifax Gentleman', written by Mrs. Craik, in which Tewkesbury was called Nortonbury and the Mill belonged to Abel Fletcher, John Halifax's boss.

TROUT ITALIANA   *Serves 4*

The George Inn was once a hostel for pilgrims to Winchcombe Abbey. Over the door are the initials of Richard Kydderminster, last Abbot of Winchcombe, who no doubt feasted on trout. Present-day visitors to the inn can enjoy this dish.

Metric		lb/oz	U.S.A.
	4 Trout, gutted and cleaned with heads left on		
1	Onion, chopped	1	1
1	Bay leaf	1	1
6	Juniper berries	6	6
225 ml	Dry white wine	8 fl. oz	½ cup
15 g	Butter	½ oz	1 tbsp
	For the sauce:		
1	Tomato	1	1
1	Small green pepper	1	1
1	Onion, finely chopped	1	1
1	Garlic clove, crushed	1	1
2 tbsp	Oil	2 tbsp	2 tbsp
1 tbsp	Flour	1 tbsp	1 tbsp

1. Set the oven to 190°C, 350°F, Gas Mark 5.
2. Arrange the trout in one layer in an ovenproof dish with the onion, bay leaf and juniper berries. Pour half the wine over, season, and dot with butter. Cover and cook for about 20 minutes until the fish is tender.

3. Meanwhile make the sauce. Blanch, skin, de-seed and chop the tomato; de-seed the pepper and chop finely. Fry the onion, garlic and pepper in the oil until soft but not browned. Add the tomato and stir in the flour to thicken the sauce. Cook gently for a few minutes, stirring all the time, then add the remaining wine and any liquid left after the trout is cooked. Re-heat.
4. Serve the trout with the sauce poured over.

Badminton

BADMINTON HOUSE, *a fine example of 17th century architecture, is part of the Beaufort estate. It is famous for its Three-Day Event, foxhunting, and the game of battledore and shuttlecock named after it.*

THE BADMINTON THREE-DAY EVENT HORSE TRIALS *began in 1949 and consist of dressage, cross country and show jumping. Princess Anne and her husband, Captain Mark Phillips, are regular competitors, and the event also attracts other members of the Royal family as spectators.*

 FOXHUNTING *is said to have begun at Badminton when the fifth Duke, after a poor day's sport with his hounds, gave chase to a fox. It gave him such a famous run that from then on foxes were hunted regularly.*

THE GAME OF BADMINTON *was invented by a later Duke, who decided to play tennis in his large picture gallery, (the dimensions of which have determined the size of badminton courts to this day). Not surprisingly, the ball damaged so many of his pictures that the Duke had to use a shuttlecock.*

SCALLOPS WITH BACON   *Serves 4*

An ideal way to serve this delicious seafood – with the flavours of the bacon and scallops complimenting one another perfectly – this recipe comes from the Cleeveway House Restaurant.

Metric		lb/oz	U.S.A.
	12 Small fresh scallops		
2 tbsp	Seasoned flour	2 tbsp	2 tbsp
60 g	Butter	2 oz	¼ cup
1	Large onion, finely chopped	1	1
4	Smoked bacon rashers, chopped and de-rinded	4	4
1	Lemon, juice of	1	1
150 ml	Double cream	¼ pt	½ cup

1. Melt the butter in a frying pan, add the onion and cook until soft but not browned. Add the bacon.
2. Roll the scallops in the flour. Add to the pan and stir well, turning them over. Add the lemon juice and cream, and season with salt and freshly ground pepper. Simmer gently until the scallops are cooked (do not overcook or they will become rubbery).
3. Serve the scallops (on a bed of rice, if liked).

BERKELEY CASTLE

Although its walls were breached in the Civil War, much of this splendid edifice, which is now open to the public, has survived, including the Great Hall, kitchens and dungeons. It has witnessed many historic events in its 800-year history, including the murder of a king — Edward II was killed here in 1327.

Desserts

"Fruits that blossom first will first be ripe."

Othello
WILLIAM SHAKESPEARE, 1564-1616

FRUIT AND BRANDY BUTTER BROCHETTES   *Serves 6*

To make these brochettes, the Corse Lawn House Hotel use 1 lb
strawberries (hulled), 2 lb pawpaw (peeled, de-seeded and cut
into chunks) and 6 Kiwi fruit (peeled and quartered). Follow
their example or use your own combination of firm fruits as
available.

Metric		lb/oz	U.S.A.
250 g	*Butter*	8 oz	1 cup
250 g	*Caster sugar*	8 oz	1 cup
90 ml	*Brandy*	3½ fl. oz	½ cup

1. Thread alternate pieces of fruit on to 6 long skewers. Turn the
   grill to high.
2. Beat the butter and sugar together until smooth and white,
   then slowly add the brandy.
3. Coat the fruit with the butter and grill for a few minutes.
   Serve on warmed plates with sizzling brandy butter poured
   over.

KIWI FRUIT WITH ALMONDS   *Serves 4-6*

To enjoy Kiwi fruit as they are served at the Close Hotel,
Tetbury, prepare them as follows. Put 300 ml (½ pt, 1 cup)
water in a pan with 125 g (4 oz, ½ cup) sugar and a cinnamon
stick. Bring to the boil and simmer for 3 minutes. Cool, and add
2-3 drops vanilla essence. Peel and slice 10 Kiwi fruit, soak in 2-
3 tbsp kirsch, then coat with the chilled syrup. Sprinkle with
toasted almonds and serve with whipped cream.

FEELING BLUE? *If so, make your way to the cliffs of the
Severn Valley, where wild woad (isaltis tinctoria) can still
be found. It was used by the early Britons to dye their
bodies blue.*

SHARON TART
Serves 6-8

Served on the Barge Semington in Gloucester Docks, this dessert features a rich-flavoured fruit from Israel which looks rather like a large orange tomato. The recipe also works well with mango if Sharon fruit are not available.

Metric		lb/oz	U.S.A.
1-2	Sharon fruit, peeled and sliced	1-2	1-2
350 g	Puff or shortcrust pastry	12 oz	2½ cups
125 ml	Soured cream or yogurt	4 oz	½ cup
150 g	Brandy butter	5 oz	½ cup
30-60 g	Crystallized ginger, chopped	1-2 oz	2 tbsp
125 ml	Double cream	4 fl. oz	½ cup
	Angelica to decorate		

1. Set the oven to 200°C, 400°F, Gas Mark 6.
2. Line a 25 cm (10″) flan case with the pastry and bake blind for 20 minutes until set and crisp. Leave to cool.
3. Beat the soured cream or yogurt into the brandy butter. Stir in the ginger and spread the mixture in the flan case.
4. Arrange the Sharon fruit slices decoratively on top. Whip the cream stiffly and pipe around the edge. Decorate with angelica 'leaves', and chill well before serving.

APRICOT BRANDY FLAN
Serves 6-8

You will need to soak dried apricots overnight to make this mouthwatering recipe from the Gloucester Cathedral Refectory. Put 225 g (8 oz, 1 cup) in boiling water, then drain and chop roughly the next morning.
1. The base is made by combining 350 g (12 oz, 2 cups) crushed plain digestive biscuits with 90 g (3 oz, ⅓ cup) melted butter and 30 g (1 oz, 1 sq) melted chocolate. Press the mixture firmly into a loose-bottomed flan tin, lining base and sides evenly, then chill for 30 minutes.
2. For the filling, whip 330 ml (½ pt, 1 cup) double cream lightly, fold in 2 tbsp apricot brandy and 125 g (4 oz, ½ cup) caster sugar, and whip until thick but not buttery. Fold in the fruit, spoon into the case, and top with toasted flaked almonds.

> THE VALE OF EVESHAM, *now in the new county of Hereford and Worcestershire, is affectionately known as the garden of England, and is famous for its delicious early season fruits and vegetables. Its orchards are planted only on the slopes of the vale, so that the winter frosts can collect in the valley, leaving the trees unharmed.*

Evesham

There are many interesting sights to be seen in this attractive market town which grew up originally, like Tewkesbury and Winchcombe, around its Abbey. The Town Hall and Market Place are Elizabethan. Walk along the High Street and note **Dresden House**, built in 1690, and owned by William Baylies, one time physician to Frederick the Great of Prussia. Also, look out for a pair of ancient **stocks**, which were removed from the town jail in the 1920's but now lie outside the Abbey precincts. Close by is the **Almonry Museum**, the former home of Evesham's Abbey Almoners. Just north of the town is Greenhill where the **Battle of Evesham** was fought in 1265. **Simon de Montfort** is said to have died here, and the place where he fell is known as Battlewell. He was buried under the Abbey High Altar, but only the Bell Tower now remains.

THE HOUSE OF COMMONS *owes much to Simon de Montfort. He summoned together an assembly from the shires which he called a 'speaking', or in his native tongue 'parlement'. This later evolved as the House of Commons.*

EVESHAM CHURCHES

St. Lawrence Church, All Saints Church, and the 16th century Bell Tower make an impressive trio grouped together amid the ruins of Evesham's once prosperous Benedictine Abbey. The monastery was founded by St. Egwine in about 700 AD. The Abbey Gate dates from 1130, and the Bell Tower was built between 1529 and 1539.

LEMON FLUMMERY   *Serves 6*

At Below Stairs in Cheltenham, this tangy delight is served in individual dishes. Each one is decorated with orange segments and angelica 'leaves' and accompanied by a brandy snap or 'langue de chat' biscuit.

Metric		lb/oz	U.S.A.
2	*Lemons, rind and juice of*	2	2
30 g	*Butter*	1 oz	2 tbsp
30 g	*Plain flour*	1 oz	¼ cup
125 g	*Caster sugar*	4 oz	½ cup
2	*Eggs, separated*	2	2

1. Put 300 ml (½ pt, 1 cup) of water into a pan and heat with the lemon juice, the grated rind and butter. Whisk in the flour, bring to the boil and stir in the sugar. Simmer for 4-5 minutes.
2. Cool slightly, then whisk in the egg yolks and leave to cool.
3. Whisk the egg whites until stiff and fold into the mixture. Serve as described above.

PORT AND PRUNE MOUSSE   *Serves 6-8*

There will be no need to 'pass the port' if you have feasted on this creamy, alcoholic treat from the Snooty Fox at Tetbury!

Metric		lb/oz	U.S.A.
	450 g (2 lb) Tinned prunes		
150 ml	*Port*	¼ pt	½ cup
300 ml	*Double cream*	½ pt	1 cup
2 tbsp	*Caster sugar*	2 tbsp	2 tbsp
	'Langue de chat' biscuits		

1. Liquidize the prunes with the port. Whip the cream and reserve a little for decoration. Fold the remainder, with the sugar, into the prune mixture. Refrigerate until set.
2. To serve, spoon into glasses, top with a rosette of cream and serve with a 'langue de chat' biscuit.

CRUSHED BRANDY MERINGUE PUDDING   *Serves 6*

From the Burleigh Court at Minchinhampton, this is an ideal dessert to concoct for unexpected guests. If you make it just before sitting down to dine, the temperature and consistency will be just right by the time you are ready for dessert.

1. Whip 600 ml (1 pt, 2½ cups) double cream, adding sugar to taste, until it stands in peaks. Fold in 3 tbsp brandy and 6 meringues broken into small pieces.
2. Turn into a glass bowl or dishes, and refrigerate.

FRENCH COFFEE MERINGUE   *Serves 4-6*

If you are making your own meringue, try this coffee flavoured variation from the Gloucester Cathedral Refectory. The 'French' touch is for adults only!

1. Whip two egg whites until stiff, then add 60 g (2 oz, ¼ cup) caster sugar and continue beating until very stiff.
2. Mix 1 tbsp instant coffee powder into 60 g (2 oz, ½ cup) sifted icing sugar and fold very gently into the egg white. Set the oven to its lowest setting, and draw two 18 cm (7") circles on silicon paper.
3. Place the paper on baking sheets and fill each circle with meringue. Then bake for up to 4 hours until completely dry.
4. Whip 300 ml (½ pt, 1 cup) double cream until stiff, and stir in 1 tbsp French brandy. To serve, sandwich the rounds together with cream.

"Look here, Steward, if this is coffee,
I want tea; but if this is tea, then I
wish for coffee."   PUNCH MAGAZINE

RICH BITTER CHOCOLATE CAKE   *Serves 6-8*

Here's how the Chef at the Greenway Hotel, Shurdington, turns an everyday chocolate cake into a festive treat. Don't worry if you haven't time to make a sponge, and have to buy one. By the time you have finished, nobody will ever know!

Metric		*lb/oz*	*U.S.A.*
	20 cm (8") Plain chocolate sponge cake		
225 g	*Apricot jam, sieved*	8 oz	⅔ cup
150 ml	*White wine*	¼ pt	½ cup
2 tbsp	*Brandy*	2 tbsp	3 tbsp
450 g	*Plain chocolate*	1 lb	16 sqs
1 tsp	*Instant coffee granules*	1 tsp	1 tsp
150 ml	*Double cream*	¼ pt	½ cup

1. Slice the chocolate sponge into three horizontally.
2. Boil the jam with the wine until reduced by half.
3. Sprinkle the brandy over the sponge slices. Ladle on enough jam mixture to make them moist but still firm. Stack them on top of one another and leave until cold.
4. Melt the chocolate in a bowl over a pan of boiling water. When smooth and shiny, add the coffee (dissolved in a tbsp of boiling water) and stir until smooth. If the mixture is too thick to pour, add a little more boiling water.
5. Ladle the chocolate over the cake, allowing it to run off so as to achieve a smooth coating. Tidy up the sides with a palette knife. Leave to cool (do not put in the refrigerator or the chocolate will sweat), then decorate with the cream, whipped until stiff.

CHOCOLATE PANCAKES WITH
CREME DE MENTHE
Serves 6

The Corse Lawn Hotel usually serve these pancakes with peppermint ice cream and a 'dribble' of crème de menthe.

Metric		lb/oz	U.S.A.
	For the pancakes:		
2	Eggs	2	2
175 ml	Milk	6 fl. oz	⅔ cup
60 g	Chocolate powder	2 oz	½ cup
2 tbsp	Caster sugar	2 tbsp	3 tbsp
15 g	Butter, melted	½ oz	1 tbsp
2 tbsp	Brandy	2 tbsp	3 tbsp
85 g	Plain flour	3 oz	⅔ cup
	Oil for frying		
	For the filling:		
150 ml	Double cream	¼ pt	½ cup
85 g	Caster sugar	3 oz	⅓ cup
4 tbsp	Crème de menthe	4 tbsp	¼ cup

1. Mix all the pancake ingredients together until smooth. Use the batter to make small, thin pancakes and cool.
2. To make the filling, whip the cream until very stiff, then carefully fold in the sugar and crème de menthe. Divide the mixture between the pancakes, reserving a little for decoration, and roll each one up. Pipe a little cream on top of each pancake and refrigerate.

PANCAKES WITH BRANDIED GINGER
Serves 4

These tasty pancakes can be enjoyed at the Bell Hotel, Tewkesbury, where the chef likes to serve them accompanied with vanilla ice cream and sprinkled with toasted almonds.

Metric		lb/oz	U.S.A.
125 g	Self-raising flour	4 oz	1 cup
1	Large egg, beaten	1	1
300 ml	Milk	½ pt	1 cup
	Oil for frying		
125 g	Butter	4 oz	½ cup
60 g	Brown sugar (preferably Muscovado)	2 oz	¼ cup
125 g	Preserved ginger, chopped	4 oz	½ cup
1 tbsp	Brandy	1 tbsp	1 tbsp

1. Sift the flour and a pinch of salt into a bowl. Add the egg and half the milk and beat till smooth. Stir in remaining milk.
2. Heat a little oil in a frying pan. Pour in 3-4 tbsp batter and swirl around to cover the base. Cook for about 2 minutes on each side. Keep warm and cook another 7 pancakes.
3. Melt the butter and sugar in a small pan, then add the ginger and brandy. Fill and roll the pancakes, serving at once.

Tetbury

Every other building here is an antique shop, but most striking is the Tolsey or Market House, built in 1655. It is supported by three rows of appealingly dumpy pillars and was used for wooltrading. Nearby is **Highgrove House**, the country home of **the Prince and Princess of Wales**.

COFFEE PARFAIT   *Serves 4-6*

Chef Bennett of the Greenway Hotel, Shurdington, recommends using rum or brandy in this dish. Either way, it's a winner!

Metric		lb/oz	U.S.A.
175 g	*Sugar*	6 oz	¾ cup
6	*Egg yolks*	6	6
1 tbsp	*Instant coffee powder*	1 tbsp	1 tbsp
425 ml	*Whipping cream*	¾ pt	1½ cups
2 tbsp	*Dark rum*	2 tbsp	3 tbsp
12	*Coffee beans*	12	12

1. Make a syrup by boiling the sugar in 85 ml (3 fl. oz, ⅓ cup) of water. Allow to cool.
2. Whisk the egg yolks in a bowl set over a pan of boiling water until thick and creamy.
3. Remove from the heat, add the coffee powder and cold syrup, whisking again until cold and fluffy. Add the rum.
4. Whip the cream and fold in, reserving some for decoration. Spread the mixture in a shallow freezer container and freeze for 6 hours or until stiff.
5. To serve, divide into portions and decorate with the remaining cream and coffee beans.

THE WESTONBIRT ARBORETUM *covers 116 acres. Founded in 1829 and famous for its autumn colours, it lies just outside Tetbury on the Bath Road.*

APRICOT AND ALMOND ROULADE   *Serves 4-6*

A subtly flavoured dessert with a light texture which makes the perfect end to any meal. This recipe comes from Burleigh Court at Minchinhampton.

Metric		lb/oz	U.S.A.
6	*Eggs, separated*	6	6
225 g	*Caster sugar*	8 oz	1 cup
	Almond essence		
30 g	*Plain flour*	1 oz	¼ cup
125 g	*Ground almonds*	4 oz	1 cup
300 ml	*Whipping cream*	½ pt	1 cup
400 g	*Sliced apricots, can of*	14 oz	14 oz
	Icing sugar for dusting		

1. Set the oven to 180°C, 350°F, Gas Mark 4. Line a Swiss roll tin with greased greaseproof paper.
2. Whisk the egg whites until firm. Beat the yolks with the sugar until light and creamy and flavour with a few drops of almond essence to taste. Sift the flour over the mixture and fold in the almonds and egg white.
3. Pour the roulade mixture into the tin and spread evenly into the corners. Bake for 20 minutes or until set and springy to the touch, but still soft.
4. Allow the roulade to shrink slightly, then turn out upside down on to greased greaseproof paper. Remove the baking paper and spread the roulade with lightly whipped cream. Arrange the drained apricots on top, reserving a few for decoration, and roll up carefully. Decorate with apricots and dust with icing sugar.

Stroud

The centre of the Cotswolds wool industry in the 15th century, Stroud stands at the junction of four streams and five valleys, like a five-pointed star. The town is also famous for **woolly mammoths**! Excavated in the nearby Cairncross and Gannicox gravel pits, their tusks and teeth are in the Town Museum.

The River Frome, which runs through the town, contained special qualities for the dyeing of cloth, and the famous **Stroud-water scarlet** cloth used in military uniforms is manufactured to this day.

A BUDDING GENIUS! *The lawn mower was invented by a Stroud man,* **Edwin Budding**, *whose 1830 patent and early machines can be seen in the museum.*

CUTTING A DASH! *The actor* **Edmund Kean** *no doubt made quite an entrance when he was married in St. Lawrence Church, Stroud in 1806. A less dashing exit was made here a year later by one Lt. Delmont — see his stone in the churchyard. He was slain in the last duel fought on English soil.*

BLACKCURRANT, LIME AND MINT SORBET   *Serves 8*

The Gentle Gardener at Tetbury has provided this unusual recipe. They recommend using a food processor if possible.

Metric		lb/oz	U.S.A.
1 kg	*Frozen blackcurrants*	2 lb	2 lb
2-3	*Mint sprigs*	2-3	2-3
275 g	*Caster sugar*	10 oz	1¼ cups
2	*Limes (or 1 large lemon), grated rind and juice of*	2	2
1 tbsp	*Double cream*	1 tbsp	1 tbsp
1	*Egg white*	1	1

1. Set the freezer or refrigerator freezer compartment to its coldest setting. (Don't forget to turn it to normal once the sorbet is made.)
2. Barely cover the blackcurrants with water, add the mint and simmer until tender. Press through a metal sieve.
3. Dissolve the sugar gently in 150 ml (¼ pt, ½ cup) water, adding the grated lime rind, then boil rapidly until the syrup reaches soft ball stage (110°C, 230°F).
4. Mix the syrup and lime juice into the sieved blackcurrants, then cool. Freeze in a plastic container until firm.
5. Put the mixture into a food processor. When softened but not melted add the cream and stiffly whisked egg white, then re-freeze. If kept for any length of time, re-process three hours before serving.

STROUD MARKET AND SHAMBLES

With its bustling hilly streets, and thriving shambles and market, a strong feeling of Stroud's industrial past can still be experienced.

MELON AND CREME DE MENTHE SORBET

Serves 6

You can make this in your refrigerator freezing section if you don't have a freezer. Turn the fridge to its coldest setting, but don't forget to turn it back afterwards! This lovely recipe comes from Twelve Suffolk Parade, Cheltenham.

1. Rub the flesh of an Ogen melon through a sieve with a wooden spoon into a pan. Add 125 g (4 oz, ½ cup) sugar and heat gently, stirring until dissolved. Stir in 2 tbsp crème de menthe and freeze in a plastic container with a tight lid until it reaches the slushy stage.
2. Whisk two egg whites stiffly and fold into the mixture. Re-freeze until firm, checking after an hour. If it has 'sunk' fluff up with a hand whisk, and continue freezing.
3. Serve in chilled glass dishes, garnished with mint leaves.

Round and about

CHIPPING SODBURY, an ancient market centre with a wide, handsome main street, and a 16th century cross, is near Badminton. Inside the Town Hall is probably the world's largest oak chest, carved out of a single oak truck, and weighing over a ton. The Town Hall itself is 15th century, but its 'Tudor style' front was added in 1858, an occasion celebrated by each child in the village being given a mug of beer and a bun!

DURSLEY was once the home of French and Flemish weavers, and **Shakespeare** is said to have passed a few months cooling his heels in Dursley after poaching Thomas Lucy's deer at Charlecote — there is a reference to a local bailiff called Vixor, who is the character Vizard in Henry IV, Part 2, Act V.

MINCHINHAMPTON is famous for the beautiful creamy stone quarried nearby, which was used for facing the interior of the **Houses of Parliament**, and with which the town's houses are decorated. Minchinhampton was once one of South Gloucestershire's chief towns. Its Market House was built on pillars in 1698, and the last Lord of the Manor at **Gatcombe Park** (now the home of **Princess Anne**) was the economist **David Ricardo**. Half a mile away, in **Hampton Fields**, stands the **Longstone**, a monolith which is said to walk magically on Midsummer's Eve.

NAILSWORTH, which still boasts many fine Georgian and Jacobean merchants' houses, was another important clothing centre. The remains of merchants' mills can be seen on the river which runs through the town. Nailsworth also has associations with the 'Supertramp' poet, **W.H. Davies**, who died in Nailsworth in 1940.

THE PERRY AND DAWES ALMSHOUSES, *one of the architectural attractions at Wotton-under-Edge, were built in 1638 for the 'Poor Men and Women of the District'. They are grouped around a courtyard with a small stone basin and tap in the centre.*

NETHER LYPIATT MANOR *is said to be haunted by a blacksmith hanged by Judge Coxe, who lived there in the seventeenth century. He promised a reprieve in exchange for a pair of iron gates — then broke his word. The gates are said to open mysteriously every 25th January!*

ROSAMUND'S GREEN *at Frampton-on-Severn is supposedly named after* **Henry II***'s famous mistress, who was born and spent her childhood at the Manor House.*

SNOWSHILL MANOR, *now a National Trust property, dates back to before the Norman Conquest.* **Charles Paget Wade** *lovingly restored the house and filled it with a variety of collections from Japanese Samurai weapons and armour to early bicycles and ships' instruments. There is also a large collection of household utensils in the house, and a model village in the grounds.*

STANTON *and* **STANWAY** *are worth visiting. While Stanton's cross is medieval, with a globe and a sundial,* **Stanway House** *has an outstanding gateway built around 1630.*

SLAD, a steeply-banked southfacing village, was the home of **Laurie Lee**, known to thousands of readers through the classic evocation of childhood in his novel, **'Cider with Rosie'**.

ULEY is a delightful village close to Dursley. Here there is a famous long barrow, called Uley Tumulus, and better known as **Hetty Pegler's Tump**, named after an 18th century landowner, when squires would wear a coat of **Uley blue** to church on Sundays, and ride to hounds on Monday in Stroudwater scarlet!

WOTTON-UNDER-EDGE, tucked literally under the edge of the long Cotswolds escarpment, still retains the atmosphere of a small wool market town. **Sir Isaac Pitman** lived in Orchard Street when he worked out his shorthand writing system. The house is marked with a plaque.

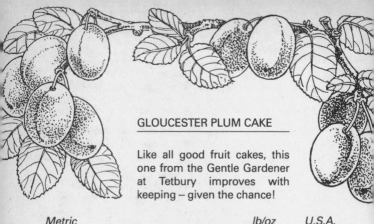

GLOUCESTER PLUM CAKE

Like all good fruit cakes, this one from the Gentle Gardener at Tetbury improves with keeping – given the chance!

Metric		lb/oz	U.S.A.
150 g	Butter	5 oz	⅔ cup
6 tbsp	Golden syrup	6 tbsp	½ cup
150 ml	Milk	¼ pt	½ cup
85 g	Chopped walnuts	3 oz	1 cup
125 g	Raisins	4 oz	⅔ cup
125 g	Currants	4 oz	⅔ cup
125 g	Sultanas	4 oz	⅔ cup
250 g	Prunes, finely chopped	8 oz	1½ cups
125 g	Mixed peel	4 oz	⅔ cup
225 g	Self-raising flour	8 oz	2 cups
2 tsp	Mixed spice	2 tsp	2 tsp
1 tsp	Nutmeg	1 tsp	1 tsp
½ tsp	Bicarbonate of soda	½ tsp	½ tsp
2	Eggs, lightly beaten	2	2

1. Put the butter, syrup, milk, nuts, fruit and peel into a pan. Heat until the butter melts, then simmer for 5 minutes. Leave until cold.
2. Set the oven to 170°C, 325°F, Gas Mark 3. Grease a 25 cm (10″) cake tin.
3. Sift the flour, spice and nutmeg into a mixing bowl with a pinch of salt. Sprinkle the bicarbonate of soda over the cooled fruit mixture, then stir it into the flour. Add the eggs and mix thoroughly.
4. Bake for 1¾ hours, covering the top with greaseproof paper for the last 30 minutes.
5. Let the cake cool for a minute or two, but remove it from the tin while still warm and *immediately* wrap in cling film or foil. Leave for as long as you can before cutting – it improves with keeping.

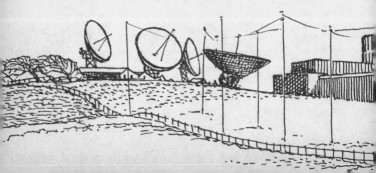

CHOCOLATE WALNUT SLICES   *Makes 12*

The cook at Thistledown in Tewkesbury is not American, but she uses a teacup to measure her ingredients in this recipe.

Metric		lb/oz	U.S.A.
125 g	Butter	4 oz	1 cup
1 cup	Sugar	1 cup	½ cup
1	Egg, beaten	1	1
1 tbsp	Cocoa powder	1 tbsp	1 tbsp
1 tsp	Baking powder	1 tsp	1 tsp
1½ cups	Plain flour	1½ cups	1½ cups
1 cup	Chopped walnuts	1 cup	1 cup
1 cup	Desiccated coconut	1 cup	1 cup
1 cup	Cornflakes	1 cup	1 cup
125 g	Plain chocolate	4 oz	4 sqs
	Chopped walnuts to decorate		

1. Set the oven to 180°C, 350°F, Gas Mark 4.
2. Cream the butter and sugar together until light and fluffy. Stir in the egg and all the dry ingredients. Press the mixture into a shallow, buttered tin and bake for 15 minutes.
3. Melt the chocolate in a basin over a pan of boiling water. When the cake has cooled, spread the chocolate over the top. Decorate with chopped walnuts and cut into 12 slices.

4000 YEARS OF SECRETS!

The General Headquarters of British Intelligence, *known colloquially as the Cheltenham spy centre, is not likely to keep its secrets as long as* **Belas Knapp**, *just a short distance away two miles south of Winchcombe. One of the most famous British long barrows, measuring 170' by 60' and 12' high, Belas Knapp was first opened in 1928. It contained 38 skeletons, including five children and a man of around 20. He belonged to the round-headed type of Stone Age man.*

ODDA'S CHAPEL *at Deerhurst, near Tewkesbury, is one of the oldest Saxon chapels in Britain, and just one of Gloucestershire's post-Roman treasures.*

ACCOMPANIMENTS

These relate to recipes earlier in the book.

Onion Marmalade

Metric		lb/oz	U.S.A.
1.5 kg	Onions, finely sliced	3¼ lb	13 cups
	Oil for frying		
275 g	Caster sugar	10 oz	1¼ cups
150 ml	Raspberry vinegar	¼ pt	½ cup
5 tbsp	Cassis (blackcurrant liqueur)	5 tbsp	½ cup
600 ml	Red wine	1 pt	2½ cups

1. Heat 3-4 tablespoons of oil in a heavy-based frying pan. Add the onions and sugar and season with salt and pepper. Cover and cook gently for 20 minutes, stirring occasionally.
2. Add the remaining ingredients and cook, uncovered, for a further 30 minutes, stirring occasionally. Cool and pour into small pots.

Prune Compôte

This is more than is needed for one occasion. The remainder will keep well in a screw-top jar in the refrigerator, and is good with pork, lamb and game dishes. Serve hot or cold.

Metric		lb/oz	U.S.A.
	500 g (1 lb) Prunes, stoned		
2	Lemons	2	2
4	Blades of mace	4	4
12	Cloves, ground	12	12
½ tsp	Allspice, ground	½ tsp	½ tsp
450 g	Sugar	1 lb	2 cups
150 ml	Cider vinegar	¼ pt	½ cup

1. Wash the prunes and cover them well with cold water and the juice of the lemons. Finely slice the lemon rind and add together with the spices. Simmer very gently for 2 hours, adding more water if necessary.
2. Add the sugar and cook for another hour.
3. Add the vinegar and boil rapidly for 5 minutes.

Choron Sauce

Metric		lb/oz	U.S.A.
6	Egg yolks	6	6
60 ml	Wine vinegar	1½ fl. oz	¼ cup
200 g	Butter	8 oz	1 cup
250 g	Tomatoes, skinned and de-seeded	8 oz	1 cup

1. Put the egg yolks and vinegar into a bowl over hot water. Mix thoroughly and stir over a gentle heat until thickened.
2. Whisk in an ounce of the butter, then continue to whisk in the remainder a little at a time until the sauce has thickened.
3. Blend or sieve the tomatoes and stir into the sauce, then season to taste. Heat through.

Hollandaise Sauce

Metric		lb/oz	U.S.A.
8 tbsp	White wine vinegar	8 tbsp	½ cup
2 tsp	Lemon juice	2 tsp	2 tsp
2 tbsp	Onion, chopped	2 tbsp	2 tbsp
1	Bay leaf	1	1
2	Blades of mace	2	2
12	Peppercorns	12	12
6	Egg yolks	6	6
250 g	Softened butter	10 oz	1¼ cups
4 tbsp	Single cream	4 tbsp	¼ cup

1. Boil the vinegar, lemon juice, onion, bay leaf, mace and peppercorns in a small pan until the liquid is reduced to about 2 tablespoons.
2. Beat the yolks in a bowl with a nut of butter and a pinch of salt until light and fluffy. Strain liquid and add to yolks.
3. Stand the bowl on top of a pan of boiling water and add the rest of the butter in small pieces, beating continuously until thick and creamy. Stir in cream and season to taste.

Velouté Sauce

Metric		lb/oz	U.S.A.
30 g	Butter	1 oz	2 tbsp
60 g	Mushrooms, chopped	2 oz	1 cup
6	Peppercorns	6	6
1 tbsp	Parsley, chopped	1 tbsp	1 tbsp
30 g	Flour	1 oz	¼ cup
300 ml	Chicken stock	⅔ pt	1¼ cups
1 tsp	Lemon juice	1 tsp	1 tsp
45 ml	Single cream	1½ fl. oz	2 tbsp

1. Melt the butter in a pan and add the mushrooms, peppercorns and parsley. Cook gently for 10 minutes.
2. Stir in the flour and cook for a few minutes without browning until the flour is cooked.
3. Gradually add the stock, stirring all the time.
4. Simmer gently until syrupy in consistency. Season to taste, and add the lemon juice and cream.

Fish Stock

Metric		lb/oz	U.S.A.
250 g	Fish trimmings, head and bones	½ lb	½ lb
1	Onion, sliced	1	1
2	Cloves	2	2
1	Bay leaf	1	1
1	Parsley sprig	1	1

Put everything in a pan with ½ litre (1 pt, 2 cups) cold water. Cover, bring to the boil and simmer: 20 minutes for small bones, 30 minutes for large. Strain and use in soups and sauces.

Index

DESSERTS

ACCOMPANIMENTS

MEASURES & CONVERSIONS

Please read the notes on measures and conversions on page 4.
The table below will help our American readers.

English	American
Bicarbonate of soda	Baking soda
Caster sugar	Fine granulated sugar
Chicory	Endive
Courgettes	Zucchini
Cornflour	Cornstarch
Demerara sugar	Soft light brown sugar
Desiccated coconut	Shredded coconut
Digestive biscuits	Graham crackers
Double cream	Heavy cream
Flaked almonds	Slivered almonds
Glacé cherries	Candied red cherries
Golden syrup	Light corn syrup
Icing sugar	Confectioners' sugar
Mixed peel	Candied peel
Plain chocolate	Semi-sweet chocolate
Redcurrant jelly	Cranberry jelly
Single cream	Light cream
Spring onions	Scallions
Streaky bacon rashers	Canadian bacon strips
Sultanas	Light raisins

RESTAURANTS & HOTELS

We would like to thank the following for their help and generosity in giving us the recipes listed below. All restaurants are in the West Cotswolds, and local telephone numbers are also provided.

BARGE SEMINGTON,   413304
(Courtyard Arts Trust), Gloucester Docks, Gloucester
Manager: Mr Scott Antony
Chef: Liz Holland
  Barge Bouillabaise, 52
  Sharon tart, 62
Luncheon: 12-2 pm (Tues, Thurs, Sun) July 14th-Sept 1st.
Open some evenings for different functions.

THE BELL HOTEL, 52 Church Street, Tewkesbury   293293
Chef: Mrs Namey Roby
  Breasts of chicken with Hawaiian sauce, 47
  Pancakes with brandied ginger, 66
Luncheon: 12-2.30 pm (7 days)
Dinner: 6.45-9.15 pm (Mon-Sat) 6.45-8.30 pm (Sun)

BELOW STAIRS, 103 The Promenade, Cheltenham   34599
Proprietor/Chef: J.B. Linton
  Hot avocado with crab, 14
  Nutty pears, 32
  Pork escalopes in mango sauce, 34
  Lamb in orange and ginger, 44
  Lemon flummery, 64
Luncheon: 12-2.30 pm (Mon-Sat) Dinner: 6-11 pm (Thurs-Sat)

THE BLACK TULIP, 99 The Promenade, Cheltenham   41234
Chef: Nigel Crump
  Snails Black Tulip style, 29
  Tropical pork, 34
Luncheon: 12-2.30 pm (7 days) Dinner: 7-10.30 pm (Mon-Sat)

BURLEIGH COURT, Minchinhampton, Stroud   Brimscombe 883804
Proprietors: Mr & Mrs Benson
  Marinated mushrooms with prawns, 14
  Crushed brandy meringue pudding, 64
  Apricot and almond roulade, 68
Luncheon: 12-1.30 pm (7 days) Dinner: 7.30-8.30 pm (Mon-Sat)

BISLEY *is just four miles south of Stroud. Close to the Church are the* Seven Springs *where a well dressing ceremony is held each Ascension Day.* **Over Court Mansion,** *which belonged to Elizabeth I, is nearby.*

CLEEVEWAY HOUSE RESTAURANT, Bishop's Cleeve   2585
Proprietor: John Marfell
  Chicken liver croûtons, 30
  Stuffed chicken breasts with Chambéry, 46
  Scallops with bacon, 60
Luncheon: 12.15-1.45 pm. Dinner: 7.15-9.45 pm (Tues-Sat)
Open occasionally for Sunday lunch and Monday evenings.

CLOSE HOTEL, 8 Long Street, Tetbury   52272
Chef: Mr. Dennison
  Vegetable and tomato terrine, 20
  Kiwi fruit with almonds, 61
Luncheon: 12.30-1.45 pm. Dinner: 7.30-9.30 pm (7 days)

CORSE LAWN HOUSE HOTEL, Corse Lawn, Gloucester   Tirley 479
Chef: Mrs. Hine
    Cold terrine of fresh crab, 15
    Hot mousseline of vegetables with Choron sauce, 20
    Tournedos of veal with Noilly Prat sauce, 40
    Fruit and brandy butter brochettes, 61
    Chocolate pancakes with crème de menthe, 66
Luncheon: 12-2 pm. Dinner: 7-10 pm (7 days)

GENTLE GARDENER HOTEL, Long Street, Tetbury   52884
Proprietress/Chef: Mrs. Knock
    Iced fennel soup with almonds, 13
    Pork fillet en croûte with prune compôte, 35
    Stuffed chicken breasts in curry sauce, 48
    Blackcurrant, lime and mint sorbet, 69
    Gloucester plum cake, 72
Bar lunches: 11-2.30 pm (Mon-Sat). 12.15-2.15 pm (Sun)
Dinner: 7.30-9.45 pm (Wed-Sat)

THE GEORGE INN, High Street, Winchcombe   602331
Chef: Mr Bill Warne
    Trout Italiana, 58
Luncheon: 12-2pm Dinner: 7-10.30 pm (7 days)

GLOUCESTER CATHEDRAL REFECTORY,   418803
Church House, College Green, Gloucester
Proprietors/Chefs: Joan Thompson, Judith Armiger
    Artichoke and tomato soup, 11, Carrot and orange soup, 12
    Gloucestershire ham bake, 33
    Apricot brandy flan, 62, French coffee meringue, 65
Open: 10-5 pm (Feb-Nov) 10-2 pm (Nov-Feb)

THE GREENWAY HOTEL, Shurdington, Nr. Cheltenham   862352
Chef: William Bennett
    Veal sweetbreads in cheese sauce, 39
    Fillet of turbot in Noilly Prat sauce, 55
    Rich bitter chocolate cake, 65, Coffee parfait, 67
Luncheon: 12.30-2 pm (Sun-Fri) Dinner: 7.30-9.30 pm (Mon-Sat)

HOTEL DE LA BERE, Southam, Nr. Cheltenham   37771
Proprietor: Miss Greenhalgh
Chef: Mr. Jackson
    Vol-au-vents de boeuf bourgeoises, 38
Luncheon: 12.30-1.45 pm (7 days) Bistro: 7.30-10.30 pm (Mon-Sat)
Restaurant: 7.30-9.45 pm (Mon-Sat) 7.30-8.45 pm (Sun)

MONTPELLIER WINE BAR & BISTRO,   527774
Bayshill Lodge, Montpellier Street, Cheltenham
Chef: Stella Skjonnemand
    Garlic bread, 15
Opening times: 12-3 pm. 6-11 pm (7 days)

PAINSWICK HOTEL, Kemps Lane, Painswick   812160
Chefs: Kevin Hooper/Mr. L.M. Donnelly
    Hot sole and trout terrine with herb sauce, 16
    Chicken and herb terrine with onion marmalade, 21
    Seafood ragôut, 54
Luncheon: 12.30-2 pm (7 days) Dinner: 7.30-9.30 pm (Mon-Sat)

QUEENS HOTEL, The Promenade, Cheltenham   514724
Chef: Jeffrey Wellbeloved
    Raspberry galantine, 29
Luncheon: 12.30-2.30 pm (7 days)
Dinner: 7-9.45 pm (Mon-Sat) 7-9.30 pm (Sun)

Continued on page 80...

Continued from page 79...

THE SNOOTY FOX HOTEL, Market Place, Tetbury — 52436
Chef: David James
  Fillet of beef Estcourt Grange, 36
  Grovewood chicken, 49
  Port and prune mousse, 64
Luncheon: 12.30-2 pm (7 days)
Dinner: 7.30-9.45 pm (Mon-Thurs) 7.30-10 pm (Fri & Sat)
    7.30-9.30 pm (Sun)

THE SWAN HOTEL, Market Street, Wotton-under-Edge — Dursley 842329
Chef: Mrs. M.P. Court
  Fillet of beef in Stilton sauce , 37
Luncheon: 12.30-2.15 pm (Mon-Fri)
Dinner: 7-10 pm (Mon-Sat). Closed Sundays.

TARA HOTEL, Upton Hill, Gloucester — 67412
Chef: David Gent
  Stilton and walnut pâté, 32
Luncheon: 12-2 pm. Dinner: 7.30-9.45 pm (7 days)

TASTERS WINE BAR, 22 London Road, Gloucester — 417556
Proprietor/Chef: Mr. Graham Ruddock
  Tomato, melon and grape vinaigrette, 28
  Spiced lamb, 42
Luncheon: 12-2.30 pm Dinner: 7-10.30 pm (Mon-Sat)

THISTLEDOWN, 59 Church Street, Tewkesbury — 292215
Proprietress/Chef: Mrs. G. Milsom
  Chocolate walnut slices, 73
Morning coffee: 10-2.30 pm Luncheon: 12-2.30 pm
Afternoon Tea: 3-5.15 pm. (Tues-Sun)
(Closed Mid December-Mid March)

TWELVE SUFFOLK PARADE, 12 Suffolk Parade, Cheltenham — 584544
Proprietor/Chef: Mr. Norman Young
  Pasta Bazilique, 28
  Melon and crème de menthe sorbet, 70
Luncheon: 12-2 pm (Tues-Fri & Sun)
Dinner: 7-10 pm (Tues-Thurs) 7-10.30 pm (Fri & Sat) Closed Mondays.

Dick Whittington and his cat took the road to London in search of fame and fortune. We think his greatest good fortune was to be born in such a fascinating and beautiful part of Britain — rich in scenic beauty with outstanding architecture of amazing variety, and steeped in history. We hope this little volume helps you to enjoy it to the full. Look out for other titles in the series on your travels.

Titles available now:

Bath   Brighton and Hove
Cambridge   Stratford-upon-Avon
Edinburgh   The Heart of the Cotswolds
Oxford   York and Harrogate

In preparation:

Covent Garden
Soho
Hampstead and Highgate
Kensington and Chelsea